PERFORMANCE MONITORING IN A PROFESSIONAL PUBLIC SERVICE

PERFORMANCE MONITORING IN A PROFESSIONAL PUBLIC SERVICE

The Case of the Careers Service

MICHAEL CARLEY

Policy Studies Institute

© **Crown copyright 1988**

All rights reserved. No part of this publication may be reproduced, stored in a retrieval system or transmitted, in any form or by any means, electronic, electrical, chemical, mechanical, optical, photocopying, recording or otherwise, without the prior permission of the Department of Employment.

PSI Publications are obtainable from all good bookshops, or by visiting the Institute at: 100 Park Village East, London NW1 3SR (01-387 2171).

Sales Representation: Pinter Publishers Ltd.

Individual and Bookshop orders to: Marston Book Services Ltd, PO Box 87, Oxford, OX4 1LB.

A CIP catalogue record of this book is available from the British Library

PSI Research Report 685

ISBN 0 85374 375 4

Laserset by Policy Studies Institute

Printed by Blackmore Press, Longmead, Shaftesbury, Dorset

Contents

Acknowledgements

1. The context of Performance Assessment in Professional Public Services   1
    Introduction: the three 'Es'   1
    Main challenges to performance assessment   4
    Experiences in performance assessment   6
    The financial management initiative   6
    Other approaches to performance indicators   12

2. The Challenge of Assessing Performance in the Careers Service   15
    Introduction   15
    The role of the careers service   16
    The potential for measuring careers service performance   19
    Client-centred guidance and the enterprise economy   24
    Intelligence and coordination: expanding roles for the careers service   26
    Conclusion   29

3. The Feasibility of Monitoring Client Satisfaction   30
    Introduction   30
    Employers as clients of the careers service   33
    YTS managing agents as clients   35
    Clients in careers education   37
    Young people as clients   39
    The assessment of satisfaction: methodological review   41
    Practical guidelines for assessment of satisfaction   43
    Conclusions   46

4. The Feasibility of Inter-Authority Comparisons Using Performance Indicators   48
    Introduction   48
    Modelling the careers service delivery system   49
    Linking inputs to outcomes   50
    Control of intervening factors   51

Using performance indicators to make inter-authority comparisons	52
Standardisation of the careers service tatsk	52
The environmental context of the service	54
Resource inputs and local funding decisions	57
Professional responses to contexts	59
Conclusions	61

5. **Measuring Careers Service Activities** — 64
   Introduction — 64
   Moving forward from the CSMR — 64
   Placement rates as potential output measures — 65
   Potential output measures from external sources — 68
   Supplementary input and activity measures — 71
   Conclusion — 73

6. **The Inspectorate: A Professional Mode of Performance Assessment** — 75
   Introduction — 75
   The role of the Careers Service Inspectorate — 76
   The inspection process — 77
   Strengthening the Inspectorate to enhance performance appraisal functions — 80

7. **Enhancing Performance Through the Careers Service Management Information System** — 83
   Introduction — 83
   Destination statistics in the information system — 83
   Local authority capacity in surveying destinations — 88
   Other sources of destination statistics — 90
   Conclusions — 92

8. **Enhancing Capacity in Monitoring Young People's Destinations** — 94
   Introduction — 94
   A development programme for destination statistics — 94
   An example of use of destination statistics — 97
   Timing of the statutory leavers' survey — 98
   Categories for destination analysis — 100
   Disaggregation by relevant variables — 101

	Other issues	103
9.	**Conclusion**	104
	Conclusions on performance measurement	105
	The Careers Service Inspectorate	105
	The careers service management information system	106

References 108

Appendices 115
- A. The objectives and methods of the study — 116
- B. Functions of local authority careers service — 123
- C. Sample destination statistics in local authorities — 124
- D. The Careers Service Management Return (CSMR) and sample output — 125
- E. Sample statutory leavers destination questionnaire — 129
- F. Sample graduate leaver questionnaire — 132
- G. Sample tables generated by FDS — 137
- H. Sample material on destination statistics from selected local authorities — 142

Acknowledgements

This report is based on research commissioned and funded by the Careers Service Branch of the Department of Employment, in 1986 and 1987.

The research would not have been possible without the kind assistance of many individuals. First, I would like to thank the numerous young people, careers teachers, school heads, employers and YTS managing agents who gave me their time.

The fieldwork was greatly assisted by a number of Principal Careers Officers (PCOs) and Assistant Principal Careers Officers (APCOs) who arranged for me to visit and observe the day-to-day operations of their careers service, both in their offices and in schools and colleges. These PCOs and APCOs were Peter Brander of Bromley, Peter Gooderson and Gaynel Munn of Humberside, Tony Temple of Oldham and John Tunnadine and John Varney of Surrey.

In particular, I wish to thank the Careers Officers and Employment Assistants, too numerous to mention, who allowed me to observe individual and group counselling sessions, and who gave me the benefit of their experience. Other Principal Careers Officers whose advice was invaluable include Pat White of ILEA, Greg Smith of Haringey, Ray Auvray of Havering, Derek Hooper of Bradford, David Cleaton of East Sussex, Colin Thompson of Surrey, Chris Roberts of Devon, Frank Robinson of Somerset, and Peter Jones of Birmingham.

I would also like to record my thanks to a number of people of the Department of Employment. These include John Dewsbury, Director of the Careers Service Branch, Roy Woodcock, Chief Inspector of the Careers Service, Derek Craze, an Inspector; and the members of the research advisory group: Ann Fort, Lynn Nash, Peter Charles, Diana Wheeler, Barbara Ballard, Paul Hayes, and Ceridwen Roberts. Particular thanks are due to Francis Butler, chairman of the group, with whom I conferred numerous times.

Michael Carley

1 The Context of Performance Assessment in Professional Public Services

Introduction: the three 'Es'

The assessment of the three Es of economy, efficiency and effectiveness in the delivery of public services, is now a main theme of public administration and set for continued attention throughout the 1990s. The programme of management reforms instigated by Mrs. Thatcher for UK central government on the advice of her first 'efficiency advisor', Lord Rayner, resulted in a Financial Management Initiative which has affected many aspects of administration in central government departments. As Sir Robert Armstrong, the outgoing head of the Home Civil Service, put it in a speech in late 1987:

> even greater prizes remain to be won when Lord Rayner's scrutiny techniques really penetrate not just the £13bn running costs of the central government machine, but the £100bn of public money spent on the huge programmes of health, social security, defence, roads, employment and training and the rest (quoted in Hennessy, 1987).

But interest in the 'three Es' is hardly confined to central government, and local government too is responding to a new political agenda by the development of what has been called a 'public service orientation'

(PSO). The PSO concept has been defined by the following propositions:
- a local authority's activities exist to provide service for the public;
- a local authority will be judged by the quality of service provided within the resources available;
- the service provided is only of real value if it is of value to those for whom it is provided;
- those for whom services are provided are customers demanding high quality service;
- quality of service demands closeness to the customer (Clarke and Stewart, 1985, p.2).

The origins of the PSO have been located in Peters and Waterman's (1982) well known management text *In Search of Excellence*. The main emphasis of the PSO in whatever guise is quality in service delivery (Rhodes, 1987).

Attempts to appraise the performance of government agencies in service delivery in a quantitative fashion is called performance measurement, usually undertaken by developing what are known output or performance indicators. The recurring assessment of performance is performance monitoring. Performance monitoring systems are orientated to administrative objectives, and can be distinguished from longer-term or academic research approaches by the fact that they must be simple, understandable, annually replicable, cost effective and within the administrative, statistical and financial capacity of the agency. Finally, the term performance assessment is used here to denote the whole area of inquiry, encompassing quantitative and qualitative approaches, and recurring and one-off attempts to assess performance of agencies and/or individual professionals.

Under the FMI, considerable progress has been reported in establishing economy and efficiency measures and especially in extending strict budgetary control over new areas of administration. Progress has also been made in performance measurement for manual services at the local authority level. More problematic however is the measurement of the quality of service delivery for the non-manual, professional services of government at both central and local levels.

The context of performance assessment

This report details a research effort designed to elucidate the challenge of performance measurement and monitoring for a particular government service, the Careers Service, which provides vocational guidance to young people. Although the case study is specific to a single service, the challenges and the lessons of performance monitoring this area will strike a familiar cord to administrators and researchers attempting to devise performance monitoring systems for many public services. This is because the political, bureaucratic and methodological constraints on monitoring which are explored in this case study are typical of a generic range of problems to be found in many professional public services.

The case study throws considerable light on the problem of performance assessment, and has two sets of wider implications:

- implications for the conduct of evaluation and performance monitoring in the public services; and
- implications for the study of youth labour markets and the school-work transition.

Given the FMI, and a general level of interest in performance measurement, it is not surprising that the Careers Service Branch (CSB) of the Department of Employment should wish to inquire as to the usefulness of the Careers Service to the clients and its cost effectiveness. To that end the CSB commissioned the PSI to review the options available for assessing performance in the delivery of Careers Services in England. A first assumption of the project is that performance assessment should be a basic and important management function for all public services offered by central and local government, and every effort should be made to devise realistic and cost-effective systems for so doing. The second assumption is that the focus of the research was on both the potential for inter-agency comparisons of performance and on means for intra-agency enhancement of performance.

More specifically the objectives of the project were to:

- determine the feasibility and potential reliability of using client satisfaction measures as indicators of performance of Careers Services, where clients were defined as young people, careers educators, YTS managing agents, and other employers; and

Performance monitoring

- review other options for appraising or enhancing the performance of the Careers Service.

Additional options reviewed were first, the development of a quantitative performance indicator system; second, the role of the existing Careers Service Inspectorate in enhanced performance assessment; and third, the further development of management information sytems for the Careers Service.

The methodology of the study consisted of literature and document review, and fieldwork in twelve local authorities in England. In four local authorities fieldwork involved intensive observation of day-to-day Careers Service activities, and in-depth interviews with clients in the four client groups and Careers Service staff at all administrative levels from Principal Careers Officers to receptionists. In eight other local authorities further interviews with Careers Service staff were carried out. The research effort had the benefit of periodic advice from a Department of Employment research advisory group.

This sort of simultaneous 'bottom-up and top-down' methodology provided a most useful approach for reviewing the potential for performance monitoring. The fieldwork, which began at the level of the client and involved considerable observation of client-professional interactions, was invaluable in mapping out the dimensions of the service, and the potential for performance monitoring. Because of the complex nature of client-professional interactions, a top-down approach, which attempted to operationalise the general objectives for the service, would have been logical but insufficient. This reaffirms that in any organisational review there is no substitute for detailed and carefully planned fieldwork.

Main challenges to performance assessment

The main challenges to performance assessment in professional public services are:

- unresolved political and professional debates over the appropriate role of services, that is, how best to respond to perceived needs;
- conflicting and sometimes irreconcilable expectations and demands on services by various client groups;

The context of performance assessment

- endemic resource constraints; and
- methodological problems in quantifying objectives and measuring performance in meeting objectives.

Certainly this study found that many of the same advantages the Careers Service brings to vocational guidance tasks in terms of multiple roles and task options, flexibility, rapid needs assessment, unraveling of the complexity of destinations available to young people, professionalism, and general bridging between education, training and employment, also proved to be disadvantageous in terms of simple, cost-effective, quantified performance monitoring, which requires clearly defined objectives, roles, tasks, and output measures. There is professional and political debate over the objectives of the Careers Service, over which are its primary clients, and over whether the needs of young people for client-centred guidance also serves the interests of what is called the 'enterprise economy'. The operational objectives and functional responses of local Careers Services proved to be too complex, diverse, and subject to local constraints and reasonable differences of opinion to allow strictly quantitative analysis of objectives. This gave rise to methodological and political concerns which could not be ignored in the research.

Methodological problems identified include:
- an inability to correlate expressed client satisfaction with either efficiency or effectiveness in service delivery;
- an inability to model the complexity of the service and thus establish a mathematical relationship, or production function, between inputs and outcomes;
- the difficulty of establishing quantitative criteria by which to judge the relative performance of the services; and
- the difficulty of isolating the influence of the service from other diverse influences on vocational maturity and career development.

A related problem is that any inter-agency performance review system would require a scheme for standardising the Careers Service task among the 96 local education authorities (LEAs) in England to allow comparisons to be made. However there are substantial differences among Careers Services as a result of socio-demographic and geographic factors, and professional responses to political constraints, which can neither be quantified nor yet be ignored in any performance appraisal. This may be typical of many decentralised service systems.

These kinds of methodological problems are not unique to the Careers Service and there do not appear to be any ready models for performance measurement in these circumstances. A review of progress in central departments under the Financial Management Initiative (FMI) served to confirm that there were no easy solutions to these problems. Most of the existing initiatives under FMI were found to be in the areas of a) budgetary control and b) senior management information systems, but not in developing quantitative measures of performance for professional or other non-manual tasks in complex social situations. Further review of the work of the Audit Commission and the National Consumer Council served to reinforce these views.

Experiences in performance assessment

A number of difficulties were thought to stand in the way of the development of a cost-effective performance indicator system for the Careers Service. Before drawing conclusions however, it seemed worth looking at other attempts at performance measurement to see whether any guidance could be taken from them. In particular it was thought that developments following from the implementation of the Financial Management Initiative might be instructive.

The financial management initiative

As part of its efficiency strategy central government, in 1982, launched the Financial Management Initiative (FMI). The initiative had a main objective of promoting in each central government department a system in which managers at all levels would have:

a) a clear view of their objectives; and means to assess, and wherever possible measure, outputs or performances in relation to those objectives;

b) well-defined responsibility for making the best use of their resources, including a critical scrutiny of output and value for money; and

c) the information (particularly about costs), the training and the access to expert advice which they needed to exercise their responsibilities effectively (CMND 8616(13) quoted in National Audit Office, 1986).

All central government departments were asked to review and enhance their systems of financial control and managerial responsibility, and to develop means for an annual review of objectives and their performance in meeting those objectives.

A useful framework for examining progress under the FMI can be taken from that used by the General Accounting Office (GAO) in the USA (Grimwood and Tomkins, 1986, p.254), who suggest three levels of the analysis of performance.

Level I (Financial and compliance)
An examination of financial transactions, accounts and reports, including an evaluation of compliance with applicable laws and regulations. (Purpose: to evaluate whether operations and resources are properly accounted for and presented in reports and whether legal requirements are being met.)

Level II (Economy and efficiency)
A review of efficiency and economy in the use of resources. (Purpose: to evaluate whether the management operates with due regard to conserving its monetary, property and human resources.)

Level III (Programme results)
A review to determine whether desired results are effectively achieved. (Purpose: to evaluate the extent to which statutory or other goals are being achieved and whether alternative methods of operation should be considered.)

A good performance monitoring system includes all three levels of analysis, and one more, which is for management informations systems which encompass levels I to III, and might be called level IV analysis. However it is not the intention here to review the progress of the FMI in its entirety, which has been done recently by a number of sources whose various citations follow, but to examine in particular progress in devising tools for level III analysis as well as progress in level IV information systems.

Performance monitoring

The main thrust of the FMI has been to develop a process of multidepartmental reviews of budgeting and to link this with the Public Expenditure Survey (PES) and White Paper. There are four component parts to this effort, which requires departments to raise and answer the following questions for the Treasury:

a) What is the system of departmental budgeting, what is the bidding process for resources, how are targets set, and where does responsibility for budgeting lie?

b) How does this system link into the PES and planning system which leads to the Public Expenditure White Paper?

c) What is the departmental performance monitoring system?

d) What is the top managment information system, is this a sound system, and how does it link back to PES?

From this list can be derived the three main developmental areas in the FMI: promotion of budgetary control, outcome measurement, and examination of management information. Unfortunately for our purposes, a number of reviews of the FMI strike home the same message, that is, that progress in the area of the extension of budgetary control and economy, i.e. levels I and II, has been useful, as have reviews of top management information systems. But in the areas of level III analysis, outcome measurement, progress is nearly non-existent. As Gray and Jenkins (1986) put it 'there are clearly difficulties with output measures which are little mentioned in the FMI departmental reviews'. Recent Treasury evidence to the House of Commons Committee of Public Accounts (1986) review of FMI notes that:

> Information on final output measures over large areas (of public sector expenditure) is not actually going to be attainable ...

Similarly the Public Finance Foundation (Beeton, 1986) reports that it cannot find a single 'satisfactory performance measure' being used to assess the governments' four main spending programmes. A representative of the Management and Personnel Office (MPO) of the Cabinet Office describes to the Public Accounts Committee (1986, p.17):

The context of performance assessment

The reason why departments are not further ahead than they are is not in any sense a lack of will, it is because the subjects are intrinsically very difficult.

Nor could any lack of will be attributed to the Careers Service Branch for its previous efforts in this regard. Given the difficulties in developing performance indicators which will be discussed in this report, it proved hardly surprising that similar difficulties exist elsewhere in central government departments, even in service delivery systems considerably more centralised than that of the Careers Service.

The progress with outcome measurement in the FMI has been summarised by the National Audit Office (1986, p.19):

> Most progress had been made in developing measures for administrative expenditure (running costs), in particular, departments with large executive functions had found it relatively easy to develop useful measures which were, typically, used as part of a management information system to compare the performance of units doing similar work. Departments were allocating resources to devising ways of assessing the impact of programme expenditure but there were inherent difficulties.

Performance measurement in terms of budgetary control under FMI is therefore well advanced. For example, DHSS's Newcastle Central Office begins with PES and the supply estimates for the next year but one from which they set out tasks and objectives for groups, in order of priority, for 153 Senior Executive Officers (SEO). Each group has an objectives/resources-/priority list. The key to the process are cost centre managers who are in control of their expenditures, an example given in number of telephone calls in peak time. These SEOs have performance targets (clearance times, accuracy in filling out forms) for quality of work insofar as it can be measured. At the next higher level they have semi- annual reviews of costs and performance. Finally, everybody has a list of objectives, agreed by immediate superiors, by which individual performance is assessed. All this is tremendously useful, but it is strictly cost-control monitoring and does not begin to tackle the outcome question.

Performance monitoring

It is in moving beyond level II that serious difficulties are found. Treasury Working Paper No. 38 (1986, p.6) has discussed some of the problems:

> There are inherent difficulties in measuring the impact of all programmes. In particular, their aims are usually broad and progress towards them is not directly measurable. Many individual programmes have multiple objectives. Although achievement of particular objectives can in many cases be measured, interpretation is a problem when policy trade-offs have to be taken into account. Another common problem is distinguishing the effect of the programme from other factors.

To this question of policy trade-offs the Parliamentary Public Accounts Committee also raised the spectre of 'contradictory or competing objectives for departments'.

Other points were made by the Treasury (House of Commons, 1986, p.6) with regard to the performance of policy divisions, in which there is an obvious parallel with the Careers Service in terms of the problem of measuring quality of advice:

> No department has yet devised a satisfactory way of measuring the output and performance of policy divisions, or the specialist staff who may support them ... The main difficulties lie in the advisory nature of this type of work. It is easy to see whether advice has been accepted, but the quality of advice, or its impact are much more difficult to assess. Executive-type activity measures are sometimes used, such as throughput, response times and targets missed.

This fallback on activity measures, or intermediate output measures such as cost per client, constitute the main results in level III analysis under the FMI. This situation is not unique to the FMI and is so common as to be almost the norm in the development of performance indicator systems. The logic behind the use of proxy measures is suggested by the Institute of Cost and Management Accountants (quoted in House of Commons, 1986, para. 170) that 'so important is the concept of outputs that even a simplistic or crude approach to this difficult area is to be preferred to none at all'. The National Audit Office (1986, p.8) noted this reliance on measures of intermediate output rather than outcome:

The context of performance assessment

In many cases it had so far proved possible to assess the effect of programmes only in terms of intermediate rather than final outputs. For example, the output of the advance factory programme would ideally be measured in terms of the additional benefit to the economy of the regions covered. In practice proxy measures, including the number and cost of jobs created or safeguarded, are used.

It is worth examining the types of intermediate output measures, as have been developed by other central departments, which might be of use in measuring performance in the Careers Service. Treasury Working Paper No. 45 (1987, p.3) gives examples of generic types of what they call 'output and performance measures' for departments involved in caseload work:

a) Throughput - number of cases dealt with.

b) Productivity - usually the average output units per person. Weights are often used to express the different types of work done in each area on a comparable basis.

c) Cost - either as resources required or charge for a service.

d) Quality of Service - such as average time taken to deliver a service.

e) Quality of Work - such as error rates.

Treasury Working Paper No. 38 (1986, p.7-8) also gives examples of possible measures for departments concerned with provision of services including health and personal social services, education, social security and employment services. Some intermediate measures used are:

a) Output measures. For example, numbers of: first degrees obtained; hospital in-patient cases treated; prescriptions dispensed; courses of dental treatment given; recipients of main social security benefits.

b) Performance indicators

   i) Client:staff ratios. For example, pupil:teacher ratios, GP list sizes. They note that the interpretation of indicators of this kind depends upon the objectives of the programme.

   ii) Indicators of effectiveness including: percentage of people entitled to a particular benefit who apply for it; average length of stay in hospital (for particular conditions); positive outcomes as

Performance monitoring

> percentage of disabled clients (Job Centre services); perinatal mortality rates.
>
> iii) Efficiency indicators (usually confined to the administration of programmes) include: claimants per staff member (Unemployment Benefit Service); in-patient cases per available bed; recurrent costs per student in higher and further education; average administrative cost per benefit payment.

While what are really indicators of throughput and client:staff ratios can help us understand 'what is going on', and are used as background information by many Careers Services, the extent to which they assess performance must be questioned. For example, in the same comments to the Public Accounts Committee, a representative of the Management and Personnel Office (House of Commons, 1986, p.12) noted 'whereas crude measures are certainly better than no measures they are not adequate measures'.

Other approaches to performance indicators

The FMI experience that progress in establishing measures of budgetary control and in developing management information systems is considerably easier than developing genuine measures of outcome is hardly unique. For example, in reviewing the NHS's performance indicator system, Pollitt (1985, p.4) concludes:

> Conceptually the package suffers from some very obvious limitations. Most strikingly, the clinical indicators lack any true outcome or effectiveness measures. Of course, this is not a particularly unusual state of affairs. The relevant literature is almost tediously insistent on the difficulty of operationalising reliable measures of this type ... Yet it must be deemed a major limitation on any set of indices which purport to measure 'performance'. Furthermore, the present package is also short on output measures.

The point could not be improved upon - to say more will only be tediously insistent. But difficulty in generating outcome indicators is insufficient cause for disregarding the necessity and benefits of performance appraisal and the most appropriate response is to examine

The context of performance assessment

areas where progress can be made. The experience of the Audit Commission (1986, p.5) is instructive:

> It is true that some things never will be measurable; but it does not follow that nothing should ever be measured. However, the cost of measuring should not exceed the value of doing so.

The Audit Commission stresses that the real first step in performance appraisal is to create an organisational culture in which performance review is seen as a challenge rather than a threat, that it is to be constructive and to open up possibilities for change and improvement in service delivery. In particular it is important to balance quantitative and qualitative information, and to assess programme results in light of local knowledge of environmental and organisational constraints:

Outputs which cannot be quantified must still be taken account of in some way, otherwise the measurable (cost) will drive out the immeasurable (quality). The art in assessing performance lies in knowing when to allow political and professional judgement to extend, or counter, the objective measures available (Audit Commission, 1986, p.8).

The Audit Commission distinguishes two kinds of performance appraisal. These have a particular relevance for conclusions which will be drawn on options for the Careers Service:

a) Monitoring looks at what is done - at what level, at what cost, with what effect and how efficiently. It involves the regular and systematic collection of data. In order for monitoring to take place, suitable criteria of measurement must be defined. It is helpful if these are quantitative, although this is not always possible.

b) Analysis looks at how things are done. Implicit in this is the idea that it might be done better in a different way. Programme analysis takes the process further and asks 'Is the service still required?', 'Can its objectives be satisfied by a different means?' Unlike monitoring, analysis of performance is likely to be an occasional and ad hoc activity which arises when officers and/or members become concerned about levels of performance. Bringing in the specialist skills of operational research, statistical analysis and social research may be valuable in more ambitious reviews. However, many reviews can be carried out more simply, without the use of any special techniques, drawing on the knowledge and experience of senior management and of the staff in the department under review (Audit Commission, 1986, p.x).

In chapters 6-8 of this report it is suggested how the CSB can and does assist local Careers Services in *analysis*, through the services of the Careers Service Inspectorate, and how strategic *monitoring* of destinations of young people can contribute to Careers Service management effectiveness.

Finally, the general literature review turned to the more specific literature of vocational guidance, which revealed intense debate over the appropriate theoretical specification of the career development process, and the role and relationship of environmental context, individual psychological factors, and professional guidance in career development. Progress in quantitative methodology over the last decade, which might help model the relationship of inputs to outcomes, seemed slight, either in specifying the dynamics of career development, or in measuring the influence of professional guidance. Quantitative approaches seem unable to operationalise vocational maturity or to specify and control intervening variables, and the conclusions of much academic research was tenuous in the extreme. Although interesting and useful in promoting general debate on the importance of vocational guidance, this literature seemed of little help in devising practical performance monitoring schemes. The most useful research approaches involved surveys and longitudinal analysis, and qualitative approaches such as participant observation and key informant interviewing to assess policy impact. This material is discussed further in the next chapter.

2 The Challenge of Assessing Performance in the Careers Service

Introduction
It is entirely reasonable that the Careers Service Branch of the Department of Employment should wish to inquire as to the usefulness of the Careers Service to the clients, and whether the service, as currently operated, produces worthwhile and visible value for money for ratepayers and taxpayers. This interest in performance appraisal is not only on the part of central government, but is reciprocated by many local Careers Services, which are part of Local Education Authorities. In fact there is a long history of attempts to gauge the usefulness of the service, or some of its activities, but little progress in so doing, at least in a quantitative manner. This chapter summarises the problems and the potential for performance measurement, all of which are explored in depth in subsequent chapters.

In general, performance measurement requires that two related questions receive positive answers. The first question asks whether agreed objectives of the service can be set out clearly and simply. Clear and agreed objectives are required to understand what the Careers Service should be doing, and to generate criteria for evaluating performance. The second question asks whether it is possible to reliably

Performance monitoring

measure the extent to which these objectives are being fulfilled. Both questions are examined in this chapter.

The role of the careers service
The 96 Careers Services in England are established within Local Education Authorities as a statutory obligation set out in sections 8-10 of the 1973 Employment and Training Act. Broad objectives for the service are set out in a (soon to be revised) Memorandum of Guidance (1980) pursuant to the 1973 Act. The broad aim of the Service is:

> to help individuals leaving full-time education to make a satisfactory transition from school or college to work.

Five more specific objectives can also be identified:

i) To ensure that pupils, students and staff of schools/colleges are fully aware of the demands that working life is likely to make on young people entering employment.

ii) To ensure that pupils and staff are fully aware of the scope and range of opportunities available to them.

iii) To help pupils and students reach informed, realistic decisions about their careers.

iv) To help young people to secure suitable employment and/or training.

v) To offer help and guidance on all problems related to securing employment.

Although each LEA runs its own Careers Service, the Secretary of State for Employment is directed to give guidance of a general character on the performance of the service. The Careers Service Branch within the Department of Employment carries out these functions on behalf of the Secretary of State.

These objectives, although straightforward in themselves, are not readily translated into specific roles or functions for Careers Services to carry out, and there has been for some time a measure of professional debate and disagreement about the primary function and appropriate role of the service. At a general level this debate is concerned with whether the service should be client-oriented, giving a service of guidance and counselling to young people, or more

The challenge of assessing performance

employment-oriented, giving a service of employer liaison and provision of placements in training and employment. The establishment of Careers Services within local education authorities tends to reinforce the former emphasis; the objectives of the Department of Employment and by implication, the Careers Service Branch, the latter emphasis. In particular, *Building Business ... not Barriers* (Command 9794, 1986) notes 'the prime aim of the Department of Employment is to encourage the development of an enterprise economy'. So there is natural and unresolved difference of opinion over the appropriate role of the Careers Service, which may hamper performance appraisal.

A related factor is that the focus of the Careers Service Branch tends to be orientated to common themes or service delivery methods across all 96 LEAs, for example, the giving of guidance interviews. Principal Careers Officers, on the other hand, are active local government officials within LEAs in service to locally elected education authority members. PCOs are involved in a broad range of political and/or organisational activities (e.g. competition for limited LEA financial resources) as well in service delivery functions. Much of the activity of PCOs is substantially related to the specific local authority context in which they work. These contexts themselves are not the same but display considerable differentiation from one local authority to the next, as might be expected. Nor are the differing contexts static but vary according to combinations of national and local pressures. In 1983 the Bolton Careers Service Policy Statement noted 'significant external changes which affected the role and the work of the Service':

i) The very great increase in levels of youth unemployment caused by the economic recession, and the disproportionate effect of the recession on the employment prospects for the less able;

ii) The increase in scale and scope of Government special measures schemes to meet the needs of the unemployed, particularly the Youth Training Scheme;

iii) An increasing emphasis on the need to foster better liaison between education, training, work and adult life, exemplified by such measures as the Technical and Vocational Education Initiative (TVEI), and the Certificate of Pre-Vocational Education (CPVE);

iv) A greater focus, through changing social attitudes, on the problems and prospects of groups disproportionately affected by higher levels of unemployment, particularly women, the handicapped, and those from ethnic minorities;
v) The establishment of careers education, guidance and counselling programmes in secondary schools;
vi) The intention to move towards the provision of a fully trained and qualified Careers Service;
vii) The increasing contribution of computer applications to careers advice and guidance.

This is a useful list, applying as it does across all LEAs. However the degree of influence of these factors varies enormously from one local authority to another, depending in part on the extent of the decline of the local manufacturing base and the local rate of unemployment. Further, as shall be explored in chapter five, measurable differences among LEAs are influenced by less tangible but no less real differences in local labour market culture and local attitudes to staying-on in education.

The range of services offered by local Careers Services, partly in response to a 'reading' of local needs, are extensive. For example, more than 30 functions of Careers Services are listed in Appendix B. These are derived from direct observation by the researcher, and there are no doubt more functions which could be added. The Bolton Careers Service Policy Statement lists 62 service objectives, offered to a broad range of clients: young people, parents, careers educators, employers and representatives of other agencies like YTS. Nor are the client groups homogeneous. Young people, for example, may be at school, in further or higher education, in YTS, or unemployed. Each client group has a different perception of what the Careers Service might do for them. Differing expectations influence both demands made on the service and satisfaction with the services provided. But, because resources are finite, not all demands can be met. Also, different client groups have conflicting expectations of the Careers Service, not all of which can be reconciled. The difficulty of defining a standardised role for the Careers Service is compounded by the fact that any package of services on offer, and their funding, is not the result of a technical

The challenge of assessing performance

decision but rather a series of professional and political decisions taken locally.

The numerous and sometimes conflicting demands on the Careers Services, and the complexity of the functional responses to those demands, pose a particular difficulty in establishing an exact and quantifiable role for the service. This is not a new problem although the rise of unemployment may have served to heighten the issue. Nine years ago a report for the Employment Directorate of the Commission of the European Communities (Sawden et al., 1978, p.72) noted:

> The debate as to whether the Careers Service should be regarded as an employment service (and, therefore, be administered nationally) or an education service has continued effectively unresolved since its creation. The original 1909 Act placed the responsibility with the branch of government responsible for employment (then the Board of Trade) but from the beginning some education authorities felt that it should be their responsibility, and the 1910 Act allowed them to provide the service. At that time an attempt was made to resolve the confusion by having local authorities responsible for guidance, with employment offices responsible for placement.

Confusion over role bedevils attempts at performance appraisal, although as will be argued, the diversity of services and activities is also a reflection of a unique strength of the Careers Service. As West and Newton (1983, p.69-70) point out:

> The biggest single problem in evaluating the effectiveness of careers guidance lies in determining the most useful criteria upon which to base measures of effectiveness ... there appear to be no universally satisfactory criteria for evaluating careers guidance.

The potential for measuring careers service performance

Broad objectives for the Careers Service can surely be agreed even if a specific set of objectives is more difficult. For example general objectives for the service are increased levels of vocational maturity in young people, appropriate placements in training and employment, and satisfied clients. But for performance measurement, objectives must be

Performance monitoring

set out in such a way that measurement can take place, that is it must be possible to ascertain the specific degree to which objectives are being met, if at all.

There are three sets of methodological problems which make a quantitative assessment of Careers Service performance difficult, and which make it virtually impossible to establish outcome measures. First, it is difficult to establish a production function which links inputs to outcomes. Second, the Careers Service is only one part of a complex network which influences the desired outcome, vocational maturity, but quantitative appraisal requires a measure of control over all these influences, which are called 'intervening variables' in social science jargon. Finally, it is reasonable to hope to assess performance in terms of client satisfactions, but for the Careers Service there is almost no way to establish if any correlation exists between expressed satisfaction and the actual efficiency or effectiveness of the service delivery for the primary client group, young people. For example, if young people expect the Careers Service 'to get them a job' they may well be dissatisfied. A related difficulty is that young people making the greatest demands on the service are least able to evaluate the quality of the service provided, because their criteria for making such an evaluation are completely undeveloped.

Where inter-authority comparisons of performance are intended, there is the additional problem of standardising the situation of one local authority to that of the next so that a 'baseline' is available from which measurements can be made. Without such a baseline, which puts each LEA on a level footing in terms of the task at hand, it is almost impossible to compare the performance of one Careers Service with another in a quantitative manner.

A wide range of factors make standardisation very difficult. The patterns of local needs are influenced by socio-demographic circumstance, local geography, the degree of economic activity and the unemployment rate, local labour market culture and local attitudes. The patterns of service response are influenced by the local rate structure and its distribution, resource allocation within the LEA and the resultant client:staff ratio of each Careers Service, local political and professional priorities, the extent of penetration of YTS as a major destination for

The challenge of assessing performance

young school leavers, the contribution of the CSB Strengthening Scheme which funds outreach workers for the unemployed, and a number of other factors. Reducing all these to a quantitative formula which would allow task standardisation does not appear possible.

A final difficulty is that Careers Services respond to needs with a complex package of input services (some or all of the 30-odd functions) and this decision (actually a long series of decisions) is based in part on professional judgements about questions for which there is no right answer, only answers which are more or less appropriate to the situation. The appropriateness of a response can be judged but not usually established in a quantitative fashion.

So not only are there difficulties in setting out an agreed role for the Careers Service but even if all concerned were to agree to a set of detailed objectives, there are profound methodological difficulties to overcome and no one has yet managed to do it. Neither academics, who have tried mightily to operationalise vocational maturity and satisfactoriness of placement, nor civil servants administering non-manual government services, whether in the UK, Canada or the USA. There are no easy answers to the difficult challenges of measuring performance in complex social situations.

There is no guidance from elsewhere on how to overcome such difficulties. As noted, progress in developing performance indicators under the Financial Management Initiative (FMI) and elsewhere is mainly confined to the establishment of increased budgetary control, or in developing management information systems. Progress in developing outcomes or output indicators for non-manual government services appears to be near nil.

A review of the academic literature on vocational guidance serves to highlight similar difficulties. This literature was critically reviewed for the Careers Service Branch in three volumes in 1980 (Clarke 1980a,b,c). A current review during this research effort reveals little further progress in overcoming either theoretical or methodological difficulties, and problems reflect epistemological debates in the social sciences generally. First, arguments about a proper role for the Careers Service are mirrored in the academic literature by bitter debates among

Performance monitoring

'theory groups' which ascribe to, and attempt to defend, their particular theoretical perspective on the dynamic of career development. For example, Vondracek et al. (1983a, p.179) suggest that 'one of the major problems in the vocational literature is the absence of theoretical formulation which deals with development in more than a superficial manner'. In particular these problems are identified:

1) key constructs in theory do not reflect the complexity of the conceptual, empirical and methodological problems to be overcome;
2) theory has accorded too little recognition to the multi-dimensional, contextual and life-span features of career development;
3) theory has not been based on 'contextually sensitive' longitudinal research; and
4) empirical findings have been ignored by theoretical researchers in vocational guidance.

Vondracek et al. stress that good theory will recognise the dynamics of career development, the importance of (local) environmental context and the influence of the relationship between individual and context. They conclude that:

> Vocational intervention should be viewed as a succession of procedures designed to assist the individual, throughout his/her life, to adapt vocational functioning to changing personal situations as well as to changing economic and contextual circumstances.

This is not unreasonable, but where Vondracek et al. propose that the failure of theory is due to a failure to 'follow acceptable scientific procedures for building a theory' they are quickly taken to task by Gottfredson (1983, p.203) for the 'lack of specificity, clarity and accuracy' in their work. Gottfredson's comments are dismissed by Vondracek et al. (1983b) as lacking 'logical analysis'. This situation is not unusual and one commentator suggests that alternative theories of career development should expect to be subject to 'a veritable fusillade of objections, complaints, and outright abuse' (Pryor, 1985, p.225). This form of debate may be of only marginal interest to the practitioner of vocational guidance, and is indicative of what is commonly known as the chasm between theory and practice in the social sciences.

Such debates between theory groups are all too common in the literature of career development and further review would serve only to document a tedious litany of claim and counter-claim as to methodological approach and epistemological and political orientation of sociologists and psychologists from differing theoretical camps. One result is attempts to develop 'mid- range' theories (Law, 1981) or 'composite theories of career development' (Pryor, 1985) which integrate one approach with another. This may be productive in so far as in many of the arguments (Vondracek et al. vs. Gottfredson, for example) there is no monopoly on the reasoned or appropriate point of view. However, for the purposes of this research the conclusions of Collin and Young (1986, p.837) from their recent review of five strands of development guidance theory seem appropriate:

> Theories about career, mediated through vocational and educational agencies, provide the basis for action in the 'real world', action which has repercussions for the individual in a world in which occupational certainties are being eroded. There is, therefore, a moral as well as an intellectual and a practical imperative that the theory which informs policy and practice is coherent, adequate, relevant and applicable. The analysis we present suggests that existing theories do not meet these demands.

Advances in research methodology which might be relevant to the performance indicator approach are at much the same state. Researchers in the positivist tradition have been totally stymied by their inability to operationalise key constructs, to model complex social sytems, and to control for innumerable intervening variables. The result is that much of the conclusions of research on vocational guidance is tenuous in the extreme and generally characterised by such a myriad of caveats that the entire purpose of the research effort seems difficult to fathom. More productive approaches may lie in surveys of young people in training and the labour market, in participant observation of the process of vocational guidance, and in the use of key informant interviews to build up a composite view of experiences of new initiatives of government intervention relating back to vocational guidance, that is, the analysis of policy impact.

Performance monitoring

Given the difficulty of modelling, measuring and aggregating individual guidance needs into a theory of career development; the dramatic influence of environmental context; and the indeterminate role of formal guidance in career development, it is not in the least surprising that the academic literature offers so little assistance in the specific task of measuring performance. Some of these problems may be intractable and may suggest a misunderstanding of the role and capabilities of social science research. Other problems may be amenable to large scale research efforts. It is very unlikely that such epistemological and methodological problems can be accounted for within the confines of a simple, annually replicable, quantitative, inter-authority performance monitoring programme. However the relative usefulness of surveys and longitudinal studies, and participant observation and key informant interviews, suggests that strengthening Careers Service Branch's already existing capabilities in research administration and inspection may be more an appropriate means to appraising performance in the Careers Service. Many of the methodological difficulties suggested are reviewed in detail in subsequent chapters.

Client-centred guidance and the enterprise economy
The options and opportunities available to young people have never been more diverse and complex. With the rise of vocationally related educational programmes, like TVEI and CPVE, this degree of complexity and thus opportunity continues to grow. Most careers decisions are now seen to involve some synthesis of information, firstly about 'self' and secondly, about the broad range of opportunities available. Ball (1984) notes that client-oriented careers education and counselling approaches assume that clients can make career decisions successfully for themselves, and that 'helping professionals' (including careers officers and careers teachers) aid individual's self understanding, assimilation of appropriate careers information, and the making of appropriate choices. In this model 'the client is enabled to function proactively and work at decisions for him or herself' (Ball, p.75). These kinds of self-managment skills, once learned, can then be deployed throughout the development of one's career, which is important, since it is generally accepted that career decision making is an on-going process over a lifetime, involving a series of (hopefully)

appropriate decisions. Neither career development theory, nor macro-economic changes in terms of the decline of manufacturing and the rise of information/service sector, support traditional views of once-and-for-all decisions about static careers. Just as the focus in education is shifting towards transferable skills (for example, in information processing) useful across a range of job descriptions, so the focus in careers guidance is shifting from an emphasis on a decision, towards an emphasis on thinking skills which can put an individual in good stead throughout the career development process. The benefits of client-centred guidance for young people are set out by Clarke (1980c) p.10:

1. improved self awareness
2. increased occupational awareness and knowledge
3. improved skill in decision-making and planning
4. improved confidence and motivation.

As institutional complexity at the transition of education to training and employment grows, it reinforces the need for the careers officer's role to be as the disinterested advisor, without particular institutional loyalties. This is commonly referred to as the 'honest broker' approach. No other approach which might be envisaged can offer nearly as much advantage to individual clients, or to the health of the economic system in the longer term.

From a human capital point of view, the benefits of a client-oriented approach to careers guidance to the longer term health of the enterprise economy are considerable. High levels of career management skills enable young people to manipulate the economic system to their benefit. It is this 'manipulation' which, when millions of individually good decisions are combined, contributes to the economic well-being of society. Young people, in this view, are not to be unthinking functionaries in industry, but skilled individuals who are able to negotiate for appropriate training, education and employment borne out of a self-confidence about their own abilities coupled to an understanding of how to make use of the economic system in their own best interests. Indeed the health of an 'enterprise economy' is entirely dependent on the aggregate of numerous extended series of good decisions made by the labour force over their career lifetime. To

Performance monitoring

assume that the content of an extended series of good decisions could somehow be guessed at and inculcated in young people by dictate, or even encouragement, would be to greatly underestimate the influence and rapidity of technical and socio-economic change between now and the year 2036, when the current crop of 16+ leavers may be thinking of retiring. Certainly current thinking in organisation theory suggests that flexibility and adaptability to unforeseen changes in the socio-technical environment will be the hallmark of successful organisations and societies. Such organisations will be staffed by people with a similar flexible, adaptable approach to socio-technical change. Client-centred guidance holds out the best possibility of Careers Service contribution to these developments.

In this view the Careers Service must be clear that it has a primary client group, young people, and a range of secondary client groups (parents, employers, YTS managing agents, etc.). While it is logically possible that the interests of any *one* young person and the interests of a secondary client may conflict, this is only true at the level of the individual, and in the short-term. At the societal level, and in the longer-term, a client-centred view also serves the best interests of the secondary client groups as well as the economic well-being of the nation. Most careers officers operate according to the client-centred principle but, as will be explored in the next chapter, confusion over the appropriate role of the service, and divergent expectations of secondary clients, may serve to challenge that this is the appropriate view and cause careers officers to be unconfident about their approach. Given the objectives for the service outlined earlier in this chapter, no other approach seems tenable.

Intelligence and coordination: expanding roles for the Careers Service
The main service function of the Careers Service is expressly intended to assist young people in a difficult transition period, away from statutory education, and in a sense, away from childhood itself, towards adulthood and the more diverse range of institutions, responsibilities and opportunities that entails. The extent of Careers Service activity is unique in two ways. First it ranges from individual service to the primary client group, young people, to services to a range of secondary

The challenge of assessing performance

client groups. In serving its client groups, the Careers Service works at the bridge between individual and societal institutions, and particularly at the critical conjuncture of education, training and employment. In this sense it is unique among organisations, which generally focus on education or training or work but not all three. Of course there is a price to pay for this broad scope: roles are hard to define, and performance is difficult to measure.

The Careers Service is also unusual (although not unique) in another way. Its range of potential influence runs from LEA service delivery at the 'coalface' level of the individual, to local policy making, to influence in the national policy debate, at which contribution can be expected to be made by CSB, PCOs and by the Institute of Careers Officers (ICO), among others. The Careers Service is also a local government function represented in central government, in this case by the CSB. In entering policy debate on matters dealing with the conjunction of education, training and employment the Careers Service is thus in a position to draw on its unique breadth of view. At the LEA level, PCOs increasingly are noting that, in the absence of clear cut proof of the usefulness of delivering guidance services, it is in the best interest of their organisations to use their unique position to provide intelligence services and coordination services to the LEA, to the local authority, and to organisations working in the local authority. To the extent that information is power, and coordination invaluable when organisations may work at dysfunctional cross-purposes, Careers Services are now using their organisational advantages to compensate for the inherent weakness of being unable to demonstrate the outcomes of vocational guidance. For example, Careers Services can be seen to be developing the following roles to complement service delivery:

Intelligence
*   Many Careers Services provide increasingly sophisticated (and computerised) destination statistics to elected members, schools, to Further Education (FE) colleges and work-related non-advanced further education planning bodies, and the Manpower Services Commission. These statistics cover 16+ leavers, lower and upper sixth form leavers, YTS leavers and FE leavers, and are

Performance monitoring

disaggreaged by sex, race, occupational or training category or educational speciality (CPVE, TVEI, types of Further Education).
* Careers Services increasingly collect, by survey, employer-related labour market information which is used by local economic development units and other agencies.
* Careers Services in metropolitan areas increasingly distribute employment placement information on a regional basis.
* Careers Services increasingly collect detailed information on the young unemployed.
* Careers Services collect information on the position of ethnic minorities in the labour market.

Coordination
* Careers Services increasingly develop and administer computerised common application procedures for young people intending to go on to YTS programmes.
* Careers Services are constantly broadening the range of their contacts with social services, housing, employers, the MSC, managing agents (singly and in groups), and with voluntary organisations. Some Careers Service now coordinate local outreach services to the unemployed.
* Careers Services are increasingly developing computerised systems for coordinating the work experience placements of young people with employers, which previously had been undertaken independently by each school.

This further development of Careers Service functions beyond vocational guidance, to the strategic functions of intelligence and coordination, works not only at the system level but greatly enhances services to both the primary and secondary client groups. Meeting individualised demands for education and training requires increased coordination between agencies providing opportunities, and experienced Careers Officers establish the web of necessary contacts to do this. For example, the development of intelligence about the 'world of work' can only come from good contacts and good relationships with employers and knowledge about their needs and circumstances, and this

The challenge of assessing performance

in turn is communicated back to young people in terms of realistic knowledge about employment opportunities. The growth of different paths to vocational maturity, for example, TVEI or CPVE, demands detailed knowledge of not only those programmes but of how they interlock in cause and effect, and cost and benefit to young people, with other developments such as YTS and sixth form colleges. Without knowledge such as this, service to clients would suffer. Conversely it is the very fact of working directly with clients, and assessing their experiences of interacting within the system, that provides an excellent grounding to the information which Careers Services can tap into for policy purposes.

Conclusion

Determining an uncontroversial set of quantifiable objectives for the Careers Service may never be possible. If such a set were to be devised, measurement problems are of such an order of difficulty that conclusions would be hedged with caveats, as is the case for much of the academic literature on the measurement of the effect of vocational guidance or the appropriateness of employment placement. While the academic contribution to the exploration of the process of vocational guidance has been helpful to an understanding of the dynamics of this process, problems in devising theory and methodology suggest that it is unlikely that reasonable criteria for developing a cost effective performance indicator system can be met for the Careers Service.

None of these points reflects negatively on the general usefulness of continuing to refine and debate the appropriate objectives for the Careers Service at national and LEA levels, nor the usefulness of local Careers Services continuing to develop methods of performance measurement and appraisal.

However, given the intractable obstacles to the quantitative assessment of inter-authority performance, a realistic assessment of the options available to CSB suggests that more value for money in performance assessment will be had from enhancing the activities of the Careers Service Inspectorate in this area, and from enhancing Careers Service intelligence functions. The latter could result from CSB/local Careers Service cooperation in surveys of young people's destinations.

3 The Feasibility of Monitoring Client Satisfaction

Introduction
There is increasing awareness of the importance of consumer evaluations of public service delivery. Indeed it seems no more than common sense to suggest that client satisfaction may be a useful measure of performance in service delivery, and the view is reinforced by the recent perceptions of citizens as consumers as opposed to unresponsive recipients of government services. Some authors go as far as to argue that client judgements may be the most important criteria in service evaluation (Wallace and Rees, 1984).

In theory, client satisfaction might prove a useful surrogate for outcome measures where they are difficult to obtain. Certainly surveys of consumer satisfaction with government services are most interesting and useful to elected members of government, and as feedback to administrators. Different levels of government sometimes undertake and publish the results of such periodic surveys (for example, Cleveland County Council, 1986). As shall be shown, a number of Careers Services themselves find it useful to ask clients whether they are satisfied with the services provided.

However, following a review of the use of such measures, Carley (1981) noted that although client satisfactions were attractive in theory they tended to be problematic in practice when used for performance assessment. This is because of possible differences between reality and perception, and because of the difficulty of ascribing meaning to responses. It is not unfeasible for clients to be dissatisfied with a perfectly adequate service because of a variety of unmet needs which that service is not designed to fulfil. For example, police services cannot make up for inadequate social service provision. Conversely, citizens may quite willingly state their feelings about services about which they in fact know little or nothing. For example, the majority of citizens might be quite satisfied with environmental health services (for example, air pollution emission regulations and inspections) which are in fact substandard and inefficient. A third problem is that citizens may express satisfaction or dissatisfaction with service performance with reference to a general orientation towards government and politics. For example, a conservative person may express that the level of police service is inadequate based on general feelings about 'law and order' rather than on his own experience of police or crime. A general rule about such misleading results is that they are possible whenever there are factors which influence perceptions other than the service under consideration.

The use of client satisfaction measures in performance monitoring for non-manual professional services must be approached with at least some caution. Past research in the USA (Stipak, 1979) was unable to demonstrate any relationship between the characteristics of local government services and citizens' evaluations of those services. A more recent review (Martin, 1986, p.190) warns that 'favourable responses by consumers to broad questions about satisfaction with services must be treated with great caution'. This is because first, the degree of satisfaction expressed by clients of a public service may be related to the degree of congruence between their expectations and their experience. Martin notes that expectations are influenced by past experience of formal and informal assistance, prior knowledge and image of the particular service, conceptions of what forms of help might be possible, and such intangible factors as feelings of self-worth. Second, judgements of satisfaction with services may be influenced by feelings about particular service officers rather than assessments of results actually achieved by the service. High ratings of satisfaction can reflect a combination of low self-esteem, low expectations, and superficial views about the personality of the Careers Officer.

Performance monitoring

On the other hand, client satisfaction measures may tap important psychological feelings that policy-makers cannot ignore. If people perceive Careers Services as poor, then that is an issue even if services are not poor by any reasonable standard. Client satisfaction measures are probably best used as one part of a parcel of assessment tools when it comes to assessing particular Careers Services, and they provide a useful 'litmus' or warning sign of some perceptual mismatch between service and client.

For these reasons it was appropriate for the Careers Service Branch to inquire as to whether the expressed satisfaction of its clients could be used in a performance monitoring system. However CSB also anticipated that there would be problems, and the research specification noted that confused perceptions about the appropriate role of the Careers Service seemed to give rise to expectations which the Careers Service was unable to fulfil. The CSB suggested that if young people expected the Careers Service to provide jobs they could be disappointed when what they recieved was useful vocational guidance coupled with a practical dose of labour market reality.

It is important to link expectations to satisfactions. This relationship is often subtle and complex. For example, one activity of the Careers Service is to promote their services to employers so that they will be aware of the existence of the Careers Service and list their employment opportunities. However, the better the Careers Services promotion the higher the expectations employers are likely to have. Conversely employers with unrealistically low expectations may be more likely to report satisfaction. In any event, the Careers Service is not only attempting to engender client satisfaction but to change clients' expectations of the service, and perhaps their perceptions of the labour market as well. Further nuances of the relationship between expectations and satisfactions are reported below.

In terms of research tasks, the main challenge in measuring clients' expectations was methodological, that is, how best to ascertain what those expectations are. For satisfactions, the main problems lay in the interpretation of the expressions of satisfaction or dissatisfaction and the use to which those results might be put. The in-depth interview with clients proved appropriate to both tasks. A summary of expectations

The feasibility of monitoring client satisfaction

and likely problems of interpretation of expressed satisfactions for the main client groups of the Careers Service follows.

Employers as clients of the careers service

The traditional role of the Careers Service has been in the provision of vocational guidance to young people. In times of buoyant youth employment this seemed appropriate. However by 1982 the CSB had published a report (Ashton et al., 1982) in the preface of which the then Head of CSB referred to the changes that were 'pushing the Careers Service towards a greater involvement in the local labour market', and towards increased liaison with employers. The changes referred to were labour market shrinkage, a dramatic increase in youth unemployment, the decline of the manufacturing sector, and an attendant growth in financial, professional and scientific services which did not involve the recruitment of great numbers of low-skilled 16 year old school leavers. Subsequently Maguire and Ashton (1983) noted that in just about all the world:

> The British service is, therefore, unique in that, although each individual service comes under the direction of the local education authority and devotes a high proportion of its resources to providing vocational guidance in schools, it is also involved in the labour market as a placement agency.

It is this multiplicity of roles and thus demands on its limited time and resources that continually proves a strength of the Careers Service in terms of the broadness of the contacts but equally a challenge to its management, to the establishment of appropriate priorities, to the evaluation of its performance, and to the satisfaction of its diverse client groups.

The range of services offered to employers has expanded in the last few years and varies from LEA to LEA. In some LEAs, or for groups of LEAs, available employment positions are circulated daily by computerised systems. ILEA's Careers Service provides this facility to surrounding local authorities in a system known as VOCAL (Vacancies on Computer for the Area of London). The City of Birmingham's YPRS (Young Person's Record System) uses the City's mainframe computer to search and match, overnight, available clients'

Performance monitoring

skills and interests with available jobs. All Careers Services offer a placement service, whether manual or computerised, and supplement this with telephone advice to employers on the meaning and relevance of various qualifications. Many Careers Services actively market their services and solicit placements for their clients by contacting employers personally or by post or telephone. Sometimes this is the result of a rolling, systematic survey of local employers, set up either by geographic area or by industrial sector. In Surrey for example, Careers Officers divide up their locality into areas and visually survey the names and addresses of employers for subsequent follow-up, which solicits not only vacancies but type of firm, size, number of employees, and skill levels of employees. One by-product of these kinds of activities is an increasingly comprehensive employers register. In Birmingham similar up-dated information on employers is regularly transmitted to the City's Economic Development Office as part of the Careers Service's intelligence function.

Many Careers Services have also taken on the co-ordination of work experience on employees' premises schemes, and are developing various computerised systems for matching young people in various schools to the placement opportunities afforded by employers at times which are appropriate to employers. Employers' satisfactions with this co-ordinative function may have mostly a negative dimension in that where it is working properly they may be unaware of the Career Service's contribution to co-ordination in the system.

However the basic expectations of most employers of the Careers Service are relatively straight-forward: to file their vacancies and to receive representations from appropriate and presentable applicants in a reasonable time following a pre-selection of applicants by the Careers Service. Satisfaction levels may indicate whether this is occuring but difficulties in interpretation are possible where a) a low unemployment rate, as in the Southeast, means that a Careers Service is unable to fill vacancies or must risk sending less than suitable applicants for interviews; b) where a change in the types of employment available has resulted in a mismatch between the skills of available applicants and the requirements of the employment opportunities on offer; c) where an initial meeting of employer needs by the Careers Service results in growing expectations; and d) where Careers Service success at time x reduces the available pool of young people at time x + 1.

Sampling for performance monitoring could also be difficult in that use of the Careers Service by employers may be intermittent or nil. Conversely if local Careers offices pre-select the sample of employers with whom they have had contact, they may be inclined to bias the sample in favour of employers with whom they have had successful dealings.

Finally, in or near metropolitan areas where travel-to-work areas cross local authority boundaries employers may deal with one or more (or even up to six) Careers Services and it may be difficult to ensure that they are able to distinguish the performance of one service from another.

These points, although not intractable, do suggest that caution would need to be exercised in interpreting employers' responses to questions eliciting their satisfactions.

YTS managing agents as clients

One dramatic if varying change in the role of Careers Service in recent times has been in the degree of interaction some Careers Services have with the Training Commission and with YTS managing agents. The local Careers Services may help the Training Commission in planning programmes and numbers of places; it publicises YTS generally and particular YTS programmes in the schools, in parent/young person evenings, and on 'YTS Conferences' held for potential school leavers; it administers the YTS application procedure and counsels young people as to appropriate placements; it may monitor young peoples' progress on YTS programmes and may offer vocational guidance again at the conclusion of the programme; and it may encourage employers to become managing agents. Of course the degree of contact between Careers Service and the Training Commission/YTS is probably proportional to the importance of YTS as a destination for 16+ leavers - in the twelve local authorities surveyed here this varied from as little as 7% to as much as 41%. In local authorities in which YTS has become the major destination, servicing YTS and liaising with the Training Commission in planning has become one of the primary functions of the Careers Service. A recent Training Commission study (Gray and

Performance monitoring

King, 1986) found that 70 per cent of the placements to YTS Mode A schemes in 1985/86 were via the Careers Service. The same study (p.19) found that 'in many firms YTS has become the main channel of entry, and in some cases the only channel, for 16 and 17 year old school leavers seeking permanent jobs'. In LEAs where YTS has superseded both 16+ employment and first year apprenticeships in importance there is considerable social and political reinforcement for the Careers Service to engage in YTS-related activity. Conversely, in areas with low rates of YTS take-up and corresponding high rates of 'staying-on' in education or going into employment, there may be pressure from parents, heads of schools and elected local authority members to play down cooperation with the Training Commission in planning and promotion of YTS, which may be perceived as a 'last choice' option.

For most managing agents, expectations of the Careers Service are about the same as employers with regard to presentable applicants. However there are three areas of complexity which may cause managing agents to hold the Careers Service responsible for factors beyond its control. The first is that in local authorities where YTS is the major destination, Careers Services have increasingly taken on the role of processing of YTS applicants and applications, even to the extent of developing computerised common application systems for so doing. Managing agents' expectations as to the sophistication and development for these systems may be unrealistic given a myriad of other constraints on the workings of the Careers Service. Second, the Careers Service tends to be client-centred with regard to young people. However, young people's best interests in terms of vocational guidance, training, and mobility between YTS programmes, and between YTS and employment, may not accord with managing agents' interests in stability of placements. Some of the managing agents interviewed clearly resented client monitoring and continued vocational counselling as an intrusion into their area of control, and expected careers officers to act as agents of YTS and not to encourage mobility, however much mobility might be in the clients' interest. Third, in areas where YTS is only of minor importance as a destination there can be intense competition among agents for young people to fill YTS programmes. Careers officers explicitly or implicitly discriminate against what they perceive as poor programmes, and a lack of applicants, for whatever

The feasibility of monitoring client satisfaction

reason, leads to managing agent dissatisfaction and may even result in the closure of YTS programmes.

In summary, considerable caution would need to be exercised in using managing agents' satisfaction ratings as a measure of Careers Service performance, at least without first specifying clearly the relationship between the two. That relationship will vary considerably depending on the importance of YTS as a destination. Sampling problems apply as with employers in terms of the problem of sample selection. Also managing agents note that they may deal with as many as six Careers Services and care would need to be taken to ensure that satisfactions expressed related to one service and not another.

Again the problem of unrealistic expectations and differing views over the appropriate role of the Careers Service may confound attempts to use expressed satisfaction as an indicator of inter-authority performance levels in service delivery.

Clients in careers education
The perceived role of the careers officer in the school may vary from that of a respected careers education team member to that of an interloper from town hall. Expectations of teachers as to careers officers' functions are complex and range from blanket to selective interviewing, option choice work, group work, curriculum development, coordination of work experience programmes and others. The greater the degree of expectation the greater the scope for dissatisfaction, especially where expectations are unreasonable or based on a poor appreciation of other constraints (e.g. budget, time etc.) operating on careers officers. Careers teachers may feel that careers officers do not spend enough time at their school, and they express concern about the turnover rate of careers officers without necessarily appreciating the salary structure, and problems like the cost of housing, which may make it difficult to fill vacancies. Personality factors also present themselves - teachers and careers officers need to 'get along' as team members, and where this does not occur only a careful assessment can ascertain wherein lies the problem. It is generally reported that it takes 2-3 years to build up a good working relationship

Performance monitoring

between careers teachers and careers officers, and where there is careers staff turnover for other reasons this affects the relationship.

Satisfactions of careers teachers may be considerably influenced by their own status or lack of it in the school, and this may in turn be dependent on the views of the head as to the role of careers education in the curriculum. Increasingly careers education has a more prominent role, with higher scale posts, better timetabling, more spacious accommodation etc. But some careers teachers still operate out of a broom cupboard during the dinner hour.

The extent and quality of careers education varies considerably. A recent survey (Cleaton, 1987) carried out for the National Association of Careers Guidance Teachers (NACGT) found that 41 per cent of careers teachers had little or no training in careers education, 60 per cent of schools had the equivalent of less than one full-time careers teacher, and 46 per cent of schools had a capitation for the careers department of less than £200 per year. In terms of time for careers education, 63 per cent of schools allocated less than 20 hours per year of fifth year curriculum time to careers education, or as the report put it (p.17) 'there is less than half an hour per week of careers education for the majority of students'. In these cases much of the careers teachers' work is done in their own time. The NACGT report concluded (p.89) 'most careers teachers feel that their work in schools is very much under-valued' and they suffer from 'lack of status'. It may prove extremely difficult to separate out feelings of insufficient status by careers teachers from their views on the satisfactoriness of the activities of careers officers.

School heads, on the other hand, are particularly concerned with declining student rolls and the possibility of school closures or amalgamations. Where this is a worry, they sometimes view the careers officer as an agent of 'outside' or competing interests, especially YTS and higher/further education. Capitation arrangements mean that a six-former is usually worth about five fifth-formers in resource terms, and heads may be very upset where a careers officer is perceived to have recommended YTS over CPVE, or a further education college over the in-house 6th form. Many careers officers indicated that they needed to tread very carefully in these areas, by calling on professional and diplomatic skills. One spoke of being accused by a head teacher of 'high-jacking' young people, others of being called 'on the carpet' with a head. Clearly these factors will influence satisfaction levels, and reinforce the view that different clients do have diverse and even conflicting expectations of the Careers Service - not all of which could be reconciled, even if resources were unlimited. Again this raises fundamental cautions about using satisfaction measures to monitor performance.

Young people as clients
For young people, both expectations and satisfactions may be a function of their level of vocational maturity or awareness. However, vocational maturity, which is a true outcome measure, is a dynamic phenomenon and one which varies on an individual basis. This makes it difficult to suggest an appropriate point in time in which a young person should be asked to express their satisfaction with the Careers Service. While vocational maturity generally will be on the increase as a young person gets older, problems of recall are likely to lead to an unreliability of responses. This problem of recall has bedeviled academic researchers attempting to operationalise and test influences on vocational maturity. For example, West and Newton (1983, p.11) in their review of research on the transation from school to work note:

> Retrospective studies involve asking individuals about events which occurred in their past or attitudes which they held in the past. The reports that people give about their past experience however, are notorious for errors of omission and distortion and such reports can therefore be of only limited value.

The degree of vocational maturity attained is deeply influenced by many factors outside of the control of the Careers Service. These intervening variables, which include psychological make-up, attitude to parents/authority, peer influence, culturally determined attitudes, and others, are difficult to control and measure, even in complex and lengthy academic research projects. Assuming that young people themselves will adequately separate out one influence from another, in terms of passing judgement on its relative importance, may be an heroic assumption.

Performance monitoring

Related to this is the fact that Careers Service guidance is one component of an influence network which consists of family, peers, neighbourhood, school, careers education and the careers service. It has proved nearly impossible to disentangle the influences of each of these on vocational maturity. The influence of the Careers Service itself is direct (on young people) and indirect (on parents, careers teachers, curriculum, educational policy, in group work, in organising YTS evenings, etc.), and young people will be unaware of indirect influence which is an increasing part of Careers Service work. Young people are sometimes unable to distinguish the Careers Service from the careers education programme, nor is there any impetus for them to do so. Indeed the inability to do so may reflect positively on the integration of the careers officer into the careers education team. The role of the Careers Service in the influence network is, to a certain extent, residual, i.e. it attempts to fill the gaps left by parents, peers, and school at a time when a full measure of vocational awareness is important. All these factors may help to explain the generally lackluster results of previous attempts to rate the influence of Careers Service assistance by asking young people to rank order the influences on the development of their vocational maturity.

Also it will be difficult to demonstrate a statistical relationship between satisfaction and either extent of Careers Service input or increase in vocational maturity. Put simply, young people with the greatest needs may consume most Careers Service resources on a per capita basis, but may be least able to make a reasoned consideration of their satisfaction with the services received. Conversely, highly focussed students, with small/easily meetable needs may register considerable satisfaction with very little in the way of service provision. In these cases levels of satisfaction cannot be demonstrated to be related to either efficiency or effectiveness but only to individual situation and perceptions.

Finally, sampling problems may arise insofar as the degree of interaction between young people and Careers Services varies from about 45 per cent coverage in LEAs with selective interviewing systems to near total coverage in blanket or comprehensive interviewing systems. The situation is made more complex in that selective interviewing depends on the availability of skilled careers teachers to undertake prior screening of those in need of a guidance interview. Obviously only the views of young people who have had some measure of direct interaction with the Careers Service would be of interest.

The assessment of satisfaction: methodological review

In spite of a general enthusiasm for assessing performance by measuring consumer satisfaction, a review of the literature on measurement techniques does not reveal much methodological progress over the last decade, and conclusions are generally tentative. Outside of the Careers Service, some of the main positive methodological reports are in measuring satisfaction with health services, particularly with services provided by GPs (Steven and Douglas, 1986) and nurses (Hurst, 1985).

Closer to the task here, the National Consumer Council (NCC, 1986) recently published guidelines on consumer assessment of local authority services. However, a listing of the services subject to assessment reveals that five of the six areas studied involved simple, manual tasks, uncontroversial service objectives, and obvious measures of success or failure in meeting objectives. These were: housing repairs, road lighting, book lending by public libraries, street cleansing and refuse collection, and some aspects of trading standards activities. In the sixth category, play and day care services for under fives, somewhat similar to the Careers Service task, consumers' views proved 'among the most difficult to evaluate systematically'. The NCC reported that 'documented progress was slight' (p. 6.26) and suggested that in this case indicators of need, and provision and cost of service, would have to suffice where 'there are no practical, reliable measures of ultimate effectiveness' (p.6.27). The NCC's experiences reinforce three points made here. First, that for some services it is not possible to derive quantitative measures of effectiveness. Second, the absence of these should not deter implementation of more modest schemes of appraisal using what quantitative cost and throughput material is available. Third, the NCC recommends that professional and objective judgements, such as those carried out by H.M. Inspectors for Education, are an appropriate means of quality appraisal. A similar theme is explored in Chapter 5.

Performance monitoring

Other reports on measuring satisfaction are more in the order of general surveys of consumer views on local services presented without interpretation (County of Cleveland, 1986; Clarke and Stewart, 1987) or with general satisfaction with living standards in different regions in the UK (Bentham, 1986). A review of thirty years of American studies of reported satisfactions with aspects of life (Larson, 1978, pp.110-11) notes the continuing lack of evidence that subjective responses can be interpreted in the same manner across social classes, across subcultural groups, across different ages, or from individual to individual. The study reports that 'if items have markedly different stimulus properties for different sampled groups, it is almost meaningless to compare scores ... between the groups'.

A second limitation is the very restricted range of generalisations that can be made from survey measures of satisfactions with non-manual tasks. Larson cautions that responses can only be taken as quick assessments in a given social situation, and no more. Another author (Martin 1986, p.197) warns that satisfaction studies, although a useful component of performance evaluation, are not amenable to rigourous interpretation, and that research on clients must be expected to be a challenging and time-consuming activity. This suggests that the non time-consuming, cost-effective, and annually replicable criteria generally holding for performance monitoring systems may be at methodological odds with the needs to approach client satisfactions with a measured and relatively long-term research programme. For this reason the most useful client satisfaction studies for the Careers Service would be either dedicated research projects on the attitudes of young people and other clients, which conform to the rigours of discipline research, or 'quick and dirty' studies by local authorities carried out with considerable local knowledge and caution as to interpretation of results. In the latter case a large number of negative responses can be taken as a warning shot across the bows of the local Careers Service.

Examples of academic studies on client attitudes to vocational guidance include Lavercombe and Fleming, 1981; Murgatroyd, 1977; and Porteous and Fisher, 1980. However, none of the work reviewed set out explicitly to measure performance of the Careers Service, but they do serve to illustrate a range of difficulties in attitude studies, particularly of young clients.

Practical guidelines for assessment of satisfaction
In spite of the range of methodological and organisational difficulties which make client satisfaction measures inappropriate in developing a league table of LEA Careers Service performance, such measures do form a useful component of an intra-authority performance monitoring system. Certainly one hallmark of effective organisations is feedback, and any feedback is better than none. Systematic and regular feedback is essential for programme review and professional development, and such monitoring can be part of a continuing review of client needs. However, given the great number of unresolved methodological pitfalls, over-elaborate systems to measure client satisfaction may not be cost-effective.

One instrument which has been developed by Careers Service Branch for assisting in the assessment of student satisfaction with guidance interviews is the 'Students' Careers Interview Follow-up Form' (SCIFF) (Bedford and Fort, 1980). Although this fell into disuse because it was developed before YTS and thus didn't cover it, the potential exists for its reformulation. SCIFF consists of a self-complete questionnaire, in which the student is to agree or disagree with a series of twenty statements about possible benefits or outcomes of the interview, and about whether those outcomes were expected or irrelevant to the student. The form is administered in the classroom between one day and four weeks after the interview. A large scale administration of SCIFF to over three thousand students in 105 schools provided baseline comparative data by which Careers Officers could assess their clients' evaluation of their interviews in terms of a broad sample of responses. This provision of a frame of reference to assess the information is a decided advantage of the SCIFF approach. A revised SCIFF may be a useful tool for Careers Services.

A number of Careers Services make use of some client satisfaction information already. For example, the Cornwall Careers Service recently joined with the Management and Business Studies Department at Cornwall College of Further and Higher Education to engage in a series of market research exercises to ascertain what various client groups thought about the Careers Service. This was both in terms of services currently available and what additional services might be offered. The series of reports generated by this exercise were used as evidence in the revision of the county policy statement on the Careers Service.

Other Careers Services, such as those in Bradford and in the London Borough of Havering, regularly ask a range of clients to comment on services provided, either by questionnaire, or face to face contact, or both. In another example the London Borough of Bromley recently surveyed young people making use of its Advanced Further Education Information System (AFEIS). No doubt there are many other examples. These four have in common that they are non-threatening, designed by management and staff working together, and used for constructive feedback and professional development.

In general, the following guidelines for assessing satisfaction are suggested:

a) Questions about satisfaction may be preceded by a question about expectations, and every question should be quite specific in reference to a particular aspect of the service provided. Questions about the Careers Service in general will seldom be of much use.

b) Self-complete questionnaires should be short. Questions should be designed to generate simple, interpretable information which has obvious face validity. A review of the methodology available suggests that commonsense may be the best guide to setting out questions and interpreting responses.

c) Where questionnaires are used there is a tendency in gauging responses to opt for four or five point Likert scales (or some variation) for response categories. These look like:

    Very satisfied
    Satisfied
    Neither Satisfied or Dissatisfied
    Dissatisfied
    Very dissatisfied.

The feasibility of monitoring client satisfaction

However, unless sophisticated analysis to test validity of responses is intended, it is probably more appropriate and useful to use simple 'yes - no - don't know' categories to the question 'are you satisfied with the following aspects of your vocational guidance? This greatly reduces problems of interpretation, and particularly the problem of 'in-between' votes. This bunching of responses in central categories is very common, and often generates a lot of meaningless information. The main purpose of a survey should be to force the client to commit themselves to an opinion and to undercover areas of client dissatisfaction, not to try and assess subtle variations in clients' perceptions

d) Any feedback is better than none, but if statistical analysis is intended the main criterion is that samples should be representative. Minimum samples of 100-150 clients are often necessary for statistical purposes.

e) Methodological problems are such that it may be hazardous to rely on a single assessment method. In Bradford, careers officers and employment assistants use a range of techniques to assess satisfaction, including questionnaire, semi-structured interview, and group discussion. In each case, expectations of clients are explored for realism and the opportunity is taken to explain to clients about the objectives of the Careers Services and the constraints under which it operates.

f) A structured questionnaire and a semi-structured interview can generate facts and experiences, and the data is open to quantitative and qualitative analysis. However interviewing may be costly, and interviewers who are not disinterested may be tempted to 'lead' the client. Clients should have the opportunity to write in their views on questionnaires.

g) Some dissatisfaction is inevitable and it may be necessary to decide on a percentage level of dissatisfaction which triggers self-appraaisal and review. Ten per cent of dissatisfied clients may be a workable point of concern.

Conclusions

The following conclusions on the measurement of expectations and satisfactions may be drawn:

1. Client expectations may be consistent or divergent from the actual objectives and constraints of the Careers Service. Satisfactions need to be related back to expectations. However, individual or aggregated satisfaction ratings cannot on the whole be correlated with either efficiency or effectiveness in service delivery, nor can they be causally related to the real outcomes of vocational guidance. Where satisfaction ratings are useful, they are best confined to particular interventions or programmes within individual local authorities.

2. The criteria by which any idividual young client will assess satisfaction may be dependent on a) affective experience, b) personality factors, or c) the contextual situation, which includes prior careers education. Accounting in a measurable way for this broad range of intervening variables is an unresolved challenge to testing the validity of measurements, and to accepting young people's satisfactions as measures of performance.

3. Satisfaction criteria may be related to developing vocational maturity, which will change over time. The timing of the assessment may alter the response, and has implications for any aggregation of responses. It may be important to learn about the role of the Careers Service in helping young people adjust their aspirations, and become more articulate about their psychological and social needs. There may need to be a longitudinal dimension to satisfaction studies, but equally client recall is a demonstrable problem.

4. Questionnaire items may be treated differently by persons of different ages, ethnic groups, and social classes. Caution and testing is indicated.

5. Satisfaction measures tell us little about individual informants, whose responses will have unique shades of meaning dictated by mood and individual reponse style and may change over time. All responses will be quick assessments given in a social sitation. They

The feasibility of monitoring client satisfaction

do not reveal deep psychological factors but rather statements about affective experience at the level of day-to-day conversation.

4 The Feasibility of Inter-authority Comparisons Using Performance Indicators

Introduction
More common than the use of client satisfaction measures as indicators of performance are attempts to devise objective, quantitative indicators of the quality of service delivery. For many people these are what springs to mind when the term performance measurement is suggested. Such performance indicators attempt to measure the results of the provision of services, often called outcomes or outputs.

The use of quantitative indicators to monitor performance in service delivery is predicated on the following assumptions:

a) that the service delivery system can be 'modelled' or reduced to a series of defined components or tasks, each of which can be 'operationalised' or measured in some way;

b) that a relationship between the inputs to the service and its outcomes, called a production function, can be established in such a way that varying the inputs results in a measurable change in outcome; and

c) that all the other factors which might affect the outcome, but which are not the service in question, can be controlled or their effect neutralised. These are called intervening variables.

Modelling the Careers Service delivery system

These assumptions can be examined in light of what is known about the Careers Service. First is the assumption that systems or sub-systems modelling is possible. Most simply a model is a likeness of something. A model is also an imitation or abstraction from reality that is intended to order and to simplify our view of that reality while still capturing its essential characteristics. In truth, simple organisational systems are easier to reduce to an abstraction and thus to model, where simplicity is defined as a limited number of objectives related to straightforward needs and a limited range of tasks designed to meet the needs. In the converse situation can be found the reason why so little progress has been made in social modelling - complex, highly interrelated social systems are very difficult to model and very difficult to reduce to the mathematical relationships required for measurement purposes. What tends to happen when one sets out to model complex systems is either the model is too simplistic, and practitioners know it does not represent anything like reality, or else the model becomes so complex that it is both untestable and unworkable within resource constraints. The history of social indicators research is littered with such cases (Carley, 1981).

The Careers Service does not represent a simple service delivery system. For example the fieldwork for this project has identified 30 important functions or services which are delivered directly or indirectly by the Careers Services in a varying mix to clients in response to an often very quick and usually efficient, needs assessment. A glance at this list of functions (in appendix B) quickly reveals the difficulty of building a general model of service function in the Careers Service. Many of these functions may have parallel or reinforcing effects on the development of vocational maturity or employment satisfaction.

Both the complexity and the interrelated effect of the service functions weigh against modelling, and in general the Careers Service does not lend itself to the kinds of functional breakdowns in which systems modelling is likely to be possible. Even in extensive academic research projects it has proved very difficult to accurately model this degree of complexity, either of young people's needs or of the outcome of vocational guidance, which may be vocational maturity or successful and satisfactory employment in the longer term. The first may be very difficult to measure, the second may be measurable but only after many years or even decades have gone by and thus present a tremendous methodological challenge. Even if one were to accept that the guidance and placement needs of young people, and outcomes of the provision of Careers Services, are measurable, there is ample evidence that it could not be done within the constraints set out for performance monitoring systems in government. Were it to be accomplished, it would be as a result of many years of dedicated social science research. Some social scientists argue that such social systems modelling is not possible.

Linking inputs to outcomes
There is a second important step to the development of performance indicators - the objectives and standards of service delivery must be classified and the actual performance indicators of outcome must be derived from this statement of objectives. For example, a Canadian performance measurement programme suggests that the process begins with an objective statement:

> This statement requires that departments divide their services into identifiable programs. An objective or output is defined for each program to serve as the target or standard against which the service will be evaluated (Metropolitan Toronto, 1986).

It is right and logical that indicators are devised from clear objectives linked to outcomes for various parts of the service delivery system. For some government services this is not difficult, particularly where a service input can be readily isolated and defined, the output quantified in some way, and quantitative link established between them. Examples where this has been done include road sweeping, road repair, refuse collection, the preparation of school dinners, the carrying out of council housing repairs, and the provision of some leisure services, each of which has been successfully modelled. However what these have in common is that they involve basically manual tasks which can be subject to detailed work measurement procedures, they have a programme of objectives which is clear and quantifiable, and they have outcomes which are visible and on the whole uncontestable. The Careers Service on the other hand, may be seen to mediate between the

The feasibility of inter-authority comparisons

environmental complexity which young people bring to the interview and the complexity of the labour market. This done with the extremely diverse package of input services described earlier. Given the cumulative complexity of the situation, gauging the relative success of the intervention poses severe methodological problems.

Where the derivation of outcome measures of performance proves impossible there is a strong tendency to fall back on input, throughput, or what are called intermediate output measures. Input measures are the resources available to processes of service delivery, for example, numbers of careers officers per unit of students at statutory school leaving age, or amounts of money available to Careers Services programmes. Throughput indicators are measures of workload or caseload, for example numbers of guidance interviews or numbers of contacts with employers. Both input and throughput measures are important increments of management information but they do not measure performance, that is they cannot be demonstrated to alter aggregate amounts of vocational maturity, or the numbers of satisfactory employment destinations. Intermediate output measures are in fact the practical substitutes for outcome or true output measures, when they are available. The concluding section of this chapter raises the question of whether any such measures are available for the Careers Service.

Control of intervening factors
There is the need to control for intervening factors which may confound efforts to measure performance. There are two levels of such intervening variables at work in the Careers Service. First, as noted earlier, the actual outcome of the service, vocational maturity or satisfactory employment or career path, is heavily influenced by a range of factors individual to each young client which are outside the control of the Careers Service, the most notable being genetic influence, self-perception, home environment, school environment, local labour market culture, and the quality of careers education.

Second, the resource base available for structuring the input package varies according to local political objectives, most of which are outside of the control of the Careers Service. This means that both the baseline case (the young persons' needs) and the intervention itself are heavily influenced by intervening variables. The strength of the intervening variables may help to explain why much of the academic research on the effectiveness or the influence of vocational guidance has proved tenuous in its conclusions. What is clear is that there is no one correct input package of vocational guidance services, but that professional opinion (which varies) and local knowledge are both important.

Using performance indicators to make inter-authority comparisons

Where inter-local authority comparisons of performance are intended, considerable caution must be exercised in so far as the question of the degree of service coverage is a professional and/or political decision, not necessarily amenable to quantitative analysis. In its simplest terms it may come down to a question of blanket interviewing (services for all) or selective interviewing (say, more services for half the potential client group, or less services but at less cost to the ratepayer). The balance of direct versus indirect influence also enters into the equation, as do decisions to leave some needs unmet (say, guidance for adults) in the face of resource constraints. It is not that these kind of balances are unamenable to appreciative policy analysis, only that it may strain methodological and political credibility to attempt to reduce them to a quantitative model.

Standardisation of the careers service task

Comparative studies of efficiency or effectiveness using performance indicators among jurisdictions will require a comparable, standardised context from which to assess the effect of different service inputs on outcomes. In other words, to make a comparison between the way one local authority delivers Careers Services and the next requires that we have a clear idea about what constitutes a good service, that we can measure the differences, and that we can equalise the task faced by each LEA so that the relative degree of success in accomplishing the task can be assessed.

In methodological terms the only alternative to standardisation as a means for controlling intervening variables is to carefully *match* study areas so that they are as alike as possible, and then to test for this degree

The feasibility of inter-authority comparisons

of 'alikeness'. Of course, the Careers Service is in fact 96 Careers Services in England and they are decidedly unmatched. In theory, standardisation holds the key, and the process has also been called 'adjustments in the analysis' or 'control through measurement' (Moser and Kalton, 1971).

Attempts have been made to develop typologies of English local authorities across a range of factors using census or other data (Webber, 1979). These typologies, making use of variations of factor or cluster analysis, have tried to group local authorities in terms of their 'alikeness' and to separate them in terms of their differences across a range of factors. The results, while interesting for the purposes of broad analysis and discussion, have not generally proved useful for making policy initiatives on an area basis, or for standardisation for performance measurement.

Probably the most work at standardisation for performance measurement purposes has been done in terms of health service districts. A recent review (Walker and Dunn, 1987, p.794) states the problem:

> One of the problems with using the national performance indicator package ... is the crudeness of the comparison between one district's performance and the other 190 districts in the country. Health authorities vary so much in size, in types of populations they serve, and in configuration of facilities, that the value and credibility of unselected interdistrict comparisons is low.

This review suggests that it may not be sufficient to attempt to group districts by one range of factors, such as socio-economic status, but that comparisons in terms of different performance (actually throughput) indicators may each require a new subgroup of districts for comparison purposes. For example, District A would be compared with B, C and D in terms of bed throughput rates and E, F and G in terms of manual staff productivity. It is certainly important to compare like with like. However, aside from the fact that the focus is mainly on throughputs, this suggestion may introduce an almost unmanageable degree of complexity into any analysis if all 190 districts are to be compared across a range of factors. Furthermore, the lessons of the use of cluster

Performance monitoring

analysis for these kinds of purposes in the 1970s is that there is almost unlimited scope for debate about the relevance of the clusters themselves, if they are intended to be used for resource allocation or for comparing performance. The evidence is that the choice of input variables to the cluster analysis almost always reflects a series of debatable value judgements, and sensitivity analysis often reveals that the arrangement of clusters is highly sensitive to indicator choice (Carley, 1981, pp.140-141).

There has been little progress in standardising the situation among the 104 Careers Services in England and Wales for any purpose. Attempts at standardisation are made more difficult by the fact that the context of each Careers Service consists of a range of socio-economic factors, such as the availability of work and the unemployment rate; and substantially different labour market cultures in which major attitudinal differences have considerable influence on Careers Service operations. Also each local Careers Service operates within the local rate structure, a political decision which directly determines the Careers Service staff to client ratio, which is the fundamental input factor to the performance equation. Finally, to the range of environmental and broad political differences, there are a detailed series of professional decisions which vary the service response from one local authority to the next according to the environmental and political context.

The environmental context of the service
It is not necessary to dwell on the range of economic, social and cultural differences between local authorities, but only to stress that these greatly influence both task and response of individual Careers Services. At the most obvious level local authorities are geographically diverse, some urban, some rural, some compact, and some large and dispersed. These factors impose constraints or costs on service delivery. Large regions, which may be poorly served by public transport, require decentralised services, multiple offices and a replication of interviewing and library facilities. Decentralised systems are more expensive in terms of capital and operating costs and this is an important environmentally-imposed constraint on the pattern of service delivery. These environmental factors are reflected in the enormous diversity of Careers Services, which range in staff size from less than 20 employees

The feasibility of inter-authority comparisons

(ten services) to between 130 and 210 staff (8 services). Numbers of schools in LEAs range from less than 20 to over 115 in a single authority. Numbers of 16+ clients range from three thousand to over fourteen thousand pupils. Expenditures per annum on Careers Services can vary from as little as £.25 million to over £7 million.

Equally diverse are local labour markets and young people's responses to labour market factors. For example, the sample destination statistics (appendix C) for some of the LEAs under study here are illustrative of the range of first destinations of young people, the propensity to 'stay-on' in education, the degree of youth employment, and the relative influence of YTS as a substitute for employment or traditional apprenticeships. YTS as a destination can be seen to range from only about 7 per cent in one LEA up to around 41 per cent in another. In the first case the YTS is about the least important destination in the LEA, in the latter the most important destination. The situation in the latter authority is related to the decline of manufacturing industry, a dramatic reduction of employment prospects and the availability of traditional apprenticeships, higher levels of unemployment, and traditional attitudes which encourage and reinforce departures from education at 16+. Where YTS is a major destination one would expect and find that the Careers Service was heavily involved in servicing YTS, in disseminating information about programmes, in developing computerised common application procedures and in coordination of activities with the Training Commission and managing agents. Of course, because resources for the Careers Service are limited, the Careers Service will to a certain extent be servicing YTS at the expense of other activities. But the main point is that the environmental context conditions Careers Services response. Standardisation of both task and response would be necessary for inter-authority comparisons of performance. The most notable examples of such standardisation are the Rate Support Grant and RAWP (Resource Allocation Working Party), but each involve only a financial response on an area basis as opposed to a service response, contentious as they may be. Standardisation among Careers Services requires the establishment of average appropriate service responses to various tasks as criteria for assessment. This may be impossible.

Performance monitoring

The situation is made more complex because quantitative factors are insufficient to describe the influence of local culture on the labour market, and the subtle interplay between cultural factors and Careers Services task and response. In a recent study of young adults in four different labour markets Ashton and Maguire (1986, p.30) note that:

> While the provision made to prepare young people for work varied from one area to another, the most important factor influencing the young adults' response to that provision was the culture of the local labour market. Without such knowledge we cannot hope to understand the differences in the way in which young adults evaluate and respond to this aspect of their education.

Ashton and Maguire describe the effect of labour market culture as 'powerful and profound' and suggest that its influence is greater than social class, the next most powerful explanatory factor. The experiences of the fieldwork here bear out this contention. For example, where there is a strong predisposition to stay on in school, combined with a lively employment scene competing for young persons' attentions, YTS is a relatively minor factor. While the PCO in this kind of local authority may come under some pressure from managing agents to encourage young people to apply, a stronger countervailing pressure to play down YTS comes from parents, heads, elected education authority members and others. Young people for whom YTS is the best destination would need to be prepared to buck anti-YTS attitudes. In this kind of local authority the PCO may be the recipient of an unstated but clear policy emphasis against YTS. In other local authorities however, YTS may be enthusiastically supported. These differences are quite independent of the political make-up of the elected education authority membership.

In a different kind of LEA, YTS has quickly replaced employment and apprenticeships as the main destination. The existence of YTS here may reinforce a strong traditional local bias against staying-on in whatever form - so strong that a young person with nine O-levels might well decide to go on YTS rather than remain in education. In this kind of LEA, young people for whom staying-on was the best option often require considerable support and encouragement to resist the pressure

The feasibility of inter-authority comparisons

from peers and parents to leave. Employers can contribute to an anti-education ethos by suggesting to third- formers, in option choice presentations in schools, that the way to get ahead in their large company is to join at 16 as a YTS trainee. They imply that those who do not, and go into a CPVE programme for example, will be considerably disadvantaged in their employment prospects. In some LEAs the situation is equally difficult for young people of Asian ethnic origin whose parents encourage staying-on against the ethos of the majority culture. Those young people who then leave education at 17 or 18 may find that YTS- related employment options are irrevocably closed to them - an unfortunate penalty for staying-on in education.

There is not the space here for a full discussion of the culture of British labour markets, or of differing attitudes to education. The main point is that an important task of all Careers Services is to respond to, and either reinforce or attempt to change, attitudes, not only of young people but of parents, teachers, employers and others. Because the Careers Service works at the contentious bridge between education, training and employment, and because of the enormous local differences in attitude towards the appropriate responses to the tensions of this transitional period, it is difficult to either devise performance measures which are valid without contextual appreciation or to propose formulae which standardise the context.

Resource inputs and local funding decisions

The Careers Service is a decentralised service system. All Careers Services are delivered locally and 83 per cent of services are funded from the local education rate. The setting of this rate is (as of this writing) a local political decision, as is the allocation of funds to competing sections of the local education authority. PCOs are not so much technical functionaries supervising a service delivery as they are local political actors, attempting to strengthen their organisations, and competing for limited resources against other political actors. They are participants in the cut and thrust of local politics and union negotiations.

The views of elected members will influence local Careers Service resources and priorities to a varying extent, and the views of members as to the importance of the Careers Service are not predictable in terms

Performance monitoring

of their political allegiance. The main resource input to the Careers Service is in staffing levels, and the staff-client ratio across the Careers Services varies by a factor of more than three. Some local authorities are better placed than others in terms of deployment of staff to meet a range of needs. Others have such a low staff-client ratio that managers must carry a client caseload as well as attend to management tasks. Some PCOs argue that post-leaving age clients from LEAs with higher (and thus worse) staff:client ratios are displaced into adjacent local authorities with more adequate service levels. It is also the case that elected members' views may influence the distribution between generic and specialist Careers Officers, particularly with regard to unemployment specialists. Nor are staff:client ratios static. In the LEAs under study here, variations in staffing levels between 1979 to 1985 ranged from -11 per cent to +35 per cent, and both extremes represent conscious political decisions.

Finally, a varying range of tasks are assigned to Careers Services by elected members. For example, some LEAs will suggest a concentration on outreach work among the unemployed. A particular issue at the moment is the extent to which the Careers Service will deliver adult guidance services. Some do this explicitly, as a matter of political priority and advertise that they do so. Others operate on the principle that they never turn anyone away but will not advertise services to adults. Others simply do not offer adult guidance services. Again some PCOs advance the argument that adults will travel to LEAs which offer guidance, thus displacing workload from one Careers Service to another.

It may well be possible to draw conclusions about the relative efficiency and effectiveness of Careers Services with high versus low staff:client ratios. But it is unlikely that attempting to devise a performance indicator system requiring standardisation across 96 LEAs would be the way to do it. A dedicated research task carried out either by the Careers Service Inspectorate or a consultant might be more appropriate evaluation procedure.

The feasibility of inter-authority comparisons

Professional responses to contexts

Whatever the degree of interest and influence of elected local education authority members, it is also the case that PCOs, senior managers, and management teams in Careers Services constantly make professional decisions across a broad range of issues for which there is no one right answer. Many of these issues are represented in the current lively and healthy debate over goals and responses which characterise the Careers Service.

Again the decentralised nature of the provision of Careers Services weighs against standardisation in that major local policy and management options affect service delivery and patterns of expenditure of resources. Particularly influential will be:

a) the extent of centralisation or decentralisation which may be a function of members' political views, or spatial factors or the PCO's professional views, or some mix. Decentralised systems require higher capital and personnel costs;

b) whether interviewing is undertaken on a comprehensive (blanket), or selective basis, which decision when combined with the initial level of resources available may dramatically alter the pattern of service delivery;

c) the activity mix, that is, the mix of the possible thirty functions (Appendix B) which the careers officers may undertake in addition to interviewing, is a matter of professional judgement, and/or political expediency;

d) given that resources are always constrained, the patterns of expenditure in each local authority on unmet needs also reflects some mix of professional judgement and political opinion.

The extent of decentralisation as a response to geographic context has already been discussed. There is another dimension to this issue which is the extent to which services are centralised or decentralised according to a combination of political or professional views. Centralisation of services can be undertaken as a means of reducing costs or promoting effective use of resources. For example, one suburban London authority has recently shut its two outlying offices and centralised operations in a single town centre office, thereby achieving economies. Conversely, other local authorities are aggressively decentralising their operations and decision-making procedures into area offices, schools and other community-based institutions. Sometimes this is a decision of the Careers Service and the LEA, sometimes the Careers Service is responding to a decentralisation programme for the entire local authority. Unless there was an obvious right answer to the appropriate degree of decentralisation, both as a management option and as a geographic response, standardisation of patterns of resource expenditure across LEAs is not possible.

There are numerous other professional debates over service options which enliven discussion but which weigh against the development of performance indicators. One of the most telling is the decision as to whether interviews will be carried out with nearly all young people of statutory school leaving age (comprehensive or blanket interviewing) or whether interviewing is carried out on a selective basis, that is either with young people who are identified by the careers teacher as requiring an interview or who request an interview. Selective interviewing assumes the existence of a good careers education programme and careers teachers to help identify those who would benefit from an interview. Comprehensive interviewing is intended to ensure that every young person has an equal opportunity to talk with a Careers Officer. Whatever the merits of the argument, given the blanket versus selective interviewing decision and variations in staff:client ratios, the time available for the initial interview in school varies from twenty to forty minutes - a factor of two. From this initial decision there are further ramifications in terms of allocation of Careers Service time to competing tasks other than interviewing.

There are also considerable variations in the activity mix, or package of inputs, and the allocation of careers officers' and employment assistants' time across the range of available functions. With the relative decline of the interview as the primary focus of Careers Service activity, and the development of a broad range of additional activities such as YTS application and work experience coordination, employer liaison, group guidance sessions, development of careers education curriculum, organisation of parents evenings and many others, the task of developing standardised work measurement procedures as prelude to performance indicator derivation has proved difficult. The main

The feasibility of inter-authority comparisons

work in this area has been attempted by LAMSAC (1986) on behalf of the Local Authorities Association. While LAMSAC report that they have made some progress in the development of predictive staffing models for manual task areas such as refuse collection and street cleaning, their attempt to do the same for the Careers Service could only encompass a quasi-systematic review of some service inputs and throughputs. For example, LAMSAC discovered that the proportion of careers officers' time apportioned to interviews and group sessions varied from 28 to 59 per cent and amount of time spent travelling varied from zero to 11 per cent. While this is of some interest, it is impossible to envisage how this data could form part of a standardisation procedure. LAMSAC itself (p.1) cautions:

> The methods used can make no assessment of 'best practice' or quality of service and the resulting figures must not be considered prescriptive in any way.

Given the constraints outlined in this report, it may well be that no further progress in developing quantitative production functions or indicators for the Careers Service is possible, either on an intra- or inter-local authority basis. Certainly, the problems of quantitative modelling and standardisation appear intractable and it may not be cost-effective for the Careers Service Branch to pursue this approach to improving performance. Other options are available, and these will be discussed in subsequent chapters.

Conclusions

1. While it is usual and laudable to attempt to develop objective performance indicators of outcome, and complement these with subjective responses or client perceptions, in the case of the Careers Services the methodological difficulties may outweigh the benefits. The results obtained may be of little use without considerable additional expenditure on specified, longer-term, research tasks, as opposed to regular, resource-efficient monitoring activities.

2. The most intractable problem in systematic monitoring of effectiveness of careers guidance lies in determining measurable objectives and the most useful criteria upon which to base measures of effectiveness. In any attempt to measure the outcome of

Performance monitoring

vocational guidance, it will be difficult to control for external factors and the complex influence network which operates on vocational maturity. There may be no methodological resolution to this problem.

3. The operational objectives and functional responses of local Careers Services are too complex, diverse, and subject to local constraints to allow strictly quantitative analysis of objectives. This gives rise to methodological and political concerns which cannot be ignored.

4. An inter-authority performance indicator system would require a scheme for standardising the base case among the 96 LEAs in England. However the sociodemographic, geographic and political constraints, and professional responses to those constraints, result in differences among Careers Services which can neither be quantified nor ignored in any performance appraisal.

5. These methodological problems are not unique to the Careers Service and there do not appear to be any ready models for performance monitoring to which one can turn. A review of progress under the FMI served to confirm that there were no easy solutions to these problems. Most of the existing initiatives under FMI were found to be in the areas of a) budgetary control and b) senior management information systems, but not in developing quantitative measures of performance in complex social situations.

6. One obvious point is that genuine monitoring of performance, as opposed to increasing budgetary control, requires the specification of the relationship of the inputs of a service to the outcomes, and this has only been accomplished where both intervention and outcome can be quantified and there are few intervening variables. Even if one were to accept that the guidance and placement needs of young people and the extent of the influence of Careers Services were measurable, there is ample evidence that the measurement task could not be done within the constraints set out for efficient performance monitoring systems in government. A second point is that monitoring systems designed for the purposes of professional development and constructive staff feedback are not generally suitable for assessment of system performance, and vice-versa.

The feasibility of inter-authority comparisons

7. Many Careers Services would like to do more in the way of performance appraisal and a number already do good work in this area. The rest of this report focuses on practical ways to enhance reviews of performance. First, the next chapter examines some quantitative measures.

8. The Careers Service Inspectorate, given certain constraints and problems, already accords closely with the appreciative, contextual performance review system which this research suggests may be the most appropriate performance evaluation tool for the Careers Service. This is discussed further in Chapter six.

9. Performance review would certainly be enhanced by the further development of the Careers Service management information system. The strength of the existing system and one main direction for development work are discussed in Chapters seven and eight.

5 Measuring Careers Service Activities

Introduction
Before going on in subsequent chapters to examine possible ways to improve performance in the Careers Service it is useful to consider whether *any* quantitative output or performance indicators are possible, and what methodological hurdles must be overcome to enable these to be implemented. The Careers Service Branch has attempted for some time to devise performance indicators relevant to the management and operation of Careers Services, and while useful input, context and activity indicators are now available, less progress has been made in divising output or performance measures. In particular two groups of output measures have been attempted: those generated entirely from the monthly statistical return, called the Careers Service Management Return (CSMR), and those dependent on other statistical sources accessible to CSB. Each group is examined in turn, and in light of the points raised in the previous chapter. In the concluding section, a number of supplementary input and activity indicators are discussed. Throughout the chapter, the discussion focuses on the usefulness and problems in using these indicators at both inter-and intra-authority levels of analysis.

Moving forward from the CSMR
In the first chapter it was noted that the tendency in implementing the Financial Management Initiative has been to move from the

Measuring Careers Service activities

enhancement of budgetary control towards management information systems at the point where further attempts to develop performance indicators became cost-ineffective. Considerable work has been undertaken by CSB, in conjunction with representatives of local Careers Services, to improve the Careers Service information system and to develop a useful replacement for the old EDS 133/134 information returns. The revised Careers Service Management Return (appendix D), now on-line and being debugged, together with the annual staffing return to CSB, appears to take the collection of Careers Service input and activity indicators as far as is practicable. PCOs and staff value the information available to them from the CSMR as it gives them a good picture of the distribution of activities related to various client groups over time. For example, numbers of interviews per month and year can be related to the numbers of small and large group guidance sessions, which when matched against the number of statutory school leavers per annum, gives a picture of the changing importance of the interview in vocational guidance. In terms of labour market activity, PCOs particularly value the CSMR table 2(a) information by which types of interventions (interview, group session, placings) can be matched to client groups (school leavers, unemployed, employed, YTS trainees), themselves disaggregated into three relevant age groups. PCOs also mentioned the usefulness of recording the numbers of YTS trainees presenting themselves for further counselling, as this gives a clue as to whether the initial counselling had been appropriate.

Placement rates as potential output measures

Useful for intra-authority monitoring, but problematic in terms of inter-authority comparisons are indicators of intermediate output derived from the CSMR, in measures of placings in jobs and YTS, and in measures of job vacancies filled.

Placings into jobs and onto YTS are recorded monthly by Careers Services in table 2(a) of the CSMR. The total number placed in jobs or YTS can be compared to measures of client stocks, for example, the total number registering as unemployed. Of course the problem of interpreting variations in unemployment rates between local authorities renders the measure inadequate for inter-authority review, but at the

Performance monitoring

LEA level it may give a feel for the 'success' of counselling and placement in helping young people to obtain training and employment.

There is one reservation with regard to a measure of placings onto YTS. Managing agents in urban areas regularly notify as many as eight or more Careers Services of vacancies, and expect anywhere from 40-90 per cent of placements to come via careers offices, with the remainder coming from direct contact between young persons and managing agents. However some of the young people who make direct contact with managing agents may have been steered towards the YTS programme by the Careers Service, although a 'placement' has not been made and there is little possibility of assessing the degree of Careers Service influence. The multiplicity and variety of contacts between managing agents and numerous Careers Services in urban areas will greatly complicate any attempt to attribute a placement to a nominated office, although presumably at the local level the meaning of the figures will be considered judiciously.

A measure of job vacancies filled is also available from CSMR. Table 2(c) requests the following information on a monthly basis for job vacancies notified to Careers Offices:

- the number of vacancies unfilled at the beginning of period,
- the number of vacancies notified in the period,
- the number of vacancies filled in the period, and
- the number of vacancies unfilled at the end of the period.

The intention is to monitor the proportion of vacancies notified directly to a Careers Service which are filled by them either directly or via other careers offices or jobcentres.

There are a number of problems which need to be recognised in using job placement rates as measures of intermediate output. First, the numerous difficulties set out in Chapter 4 would need to be overcome. For example, there will be problems of distinguishing a local degree of effectiveness where Careers Service boundaries overlap travel-to-work areas, very common in the urban areas; problems of higher effectiveness at time x reducing the available pool of placable young people at time x+1, and problems of allowing for differential youth unemployment rates and considerable variation in the workings of local labour markets.

Filling job vacancies may be relatively more difficult in LEAs with low unemployment rates. Equally there may be a skills mismatch between those of available young people and employers' requirements. This is not something which can be laid at the door of a Careers Service, at least not completely nor in the short term, but at the intra-authority level it presents no particular difficulty beyond the need to be recognised as a constraining factor.

There is also the problem that there needs to be an operational definition of what constitutes a filled vacancy. There is considerable concern over whether 'a placing' is taken to be made successfully at the point of a client entering employment, or whether an appropriate time lapse is necessary to minimise the effect of drop-out rates on the figures. High vacancy filling rates can be coupled to high drop-out rates, and in this case it would be hard to argue that the rate of initial vacancy fillings was a guide to effectiveness. There is a danger than an emphasis on the quantity of vacancies filled at the expense of the quality of placements can result in a disservice to both young persons and employers.

There is an additional problem with measuring vacancies filled in that a careers office could be tempted to 'screen' the notifications it is willing to accept, thus increasing its chances of filling vacancies. Similarly, an office which receives few notifications, perhaps because of a poor track record with employers, will appear to perform well in filling a high proportion of those vacancies received. An attempt to account for this has led to the suggestion for a 'modified job vacancy filling indicator' which compares vacancies notified to a careers office as a proportion of those notified to jobcentres in the same locality over the same period. However, the policy changes in 1987 which will limit the role of jobcentres as placement agencies may limit or even negate completely the usefulness of this approach. In any event, it takes no account of possible variability between jobcentres themselves, which may be due to factors other than local labour market variation.

Finally it must be stressed again that measures useful at the local level are extremely problematic in terms of rigourous inter-authority comparisons. For example, if performance review was to come from an analysis of placements it would probably be necessary for Careers Service Inspectors to regularly 'audit' and test the procedures by which the CSMR was completed. However, in a very decentralised service system like the Careers Service, with 96 sub-units, this could be an expensive exercise.

There is a final reservation in that an emphasis on placings as a measure of inter-authority performance may engender poor reporting practices, and reduce valuable LEA-CSB cooperation in data collection. Of course the numbers of placements and changes in placement rates are of considerable interest to PCOs for intra-authority analysis, and many already use CSMR- generated data for that purpose. For example, one local Careers Service found in a review of its four sub-divisions that one had a far lower placement rate than the others. Administrative inefficiencies were identified and the problem rectified. However, numerous problems arise in attempting to extend this type of analysis to inter-authority comparisons. It is probably more appropriate to view the levels of job and YTS placements and job vacancies filled as context rather than performance indicators at the inter-LEA level. This would be in keeping with the recommendation of Knapp et al. (1986, p.44) that vacancy figures are important context indicators in their own right, and one which the Careers Service can provide from within its own management information system.

Potential output measures from external sources
In addition to the 'modified' job vacancy indicator examined above, the following output indicators from alternative statistical sources have been proposed:

Proportion of unemployed under 18 claiming benefit.

Proportion of unemployed under 18s registered with the Careers Service.

Success in the 'Christmas Undertaking'.

Termination indicator for YTS.

The last named could be taken as a possible extension to the YTS vacancy filling indicator. This is to measure the numbers of premature terminations from YTS as a proportion of all those starting on a scheme, and to make the assumption that a high level of premature terminations reflects on the 'nominated' Careers Service for a scheme. However, as with low placements in the YTS placing indicator, there may be good

Measuring Careers Service activities

reasons for termination, particularly as it is common for young people to move off YTS into permanent employment. It is also difficult to envisage how a premature termination could be negatively attributed to a Careers Service, without first making some judgement as to whether the YTS programme itself was substandard or unsuitable in some way.

Less problematic is the indicator which measures the extent to which each Careers Service has met the 'Christmas Undertaking', which is to make an offer of a YTS place to each potential 15+ school leaver by the Christmas after leaving. The only reservation is that all Careers Services might do equally well, since the undertaking is generally met. It is none the less important for that, and in the few cases where it is not met it may be as much an indication of the quality of the Training Commission forecasting of YTS placement needs, as a reflection on Careers Service performance.

Closest perhaps to true output indicators for the Careers Service are the two measures which focus on the unemployed under-18 year olds, claiming benefit, and who may be registered with the Careers Service. The monitoring of the proportion of these young people who are registered with the Careers Service, and by implication those who are not, presents a few methodological problems. A comparative base can be had from the small area unemployment statistics available via the National Online Manpower Information System (NOMIS). A high proportion of non-registrants may reflect on Careers Service performance. However, it will also reflect local political priorities and the funds made available to PCOs for relatively expensive 'outreach' work with the young unemployed, and once again problems arise at the inter-authority level.

It would not be unreasonable for some PCOs to argue that as much as they would like to assign staff to do more outreach work, it is expensive on per-capita basis and their priorities must lie elsewhere. It is also the case that it may be impossible to 'standardize' the task across LEAs. Where youth unemployment is relatively low, Careers Services will appear to perform well without needing to allocate resources to these unemployed clients. Conversely, in LEAS where unemployment is high, and/or with a high proportion of ethnic minority people, not only will more outreach work be required but the demands on scarce

Performance monitoring

resources may be proportionally greater. In this sense, any indicator focussed on the unemployed under 18s *may* reflect Careers Service performance, but may also carry an inherent bias against inner city LEAs and those with high rates of unemployment. However, none of these problems negate the value of the measure for monitoring within a local authority.

This applies equally to the indicator 'proportion of under 18s claiming benefit', as compared to the total population of under 18s in employment. The logic behind this proposal is straightforward and probably incontestable - that given the option of YTS attendance, the Career Service has a responsibility to reduce to a minimum the number of unemployed young people. This is an attractive option as a performance indicator, but not without problems. First, the total number of under 18 year olds in employment appears not to be available and a proxy must be found. Second, the indicator has to be predicated on the availability of sufficient, and appropriate, YTS places in each LEA. There is concern that the recently announced JTS programme will reduce the availaibility of YTS placements but it is probably too early to measure the extent of this. In mainly rural LEAs, and in areas of high unemployment, there may be insufficient numbers and variety of YTS places, particularly if a major employer has recently closed down. Third, it may be that there is a time lag in the response of supply of YTS places to demand - at least one year is obvious.

For each of these measures the question of local variation arises in assessing the potential for inter-LEA comparability. As mentioned above the degree of outreach work a service engages in is very much a function of policy and resources, and where the challenge is greatest so are the range of needs most broad. It may be unfair not to take these kinds of variations into account. It may also be necessary to 'correct' for the base youth unemployment rate and for the operations of the local labour market, but it is hard to envision how exactly to allow for this factor. For example, in the Southeast young people might reasonably remain unemployed for a period while scanning the lively job market. Equally difficult will be to account for those young people collecting benefit but attending college under the DHSS's '12 or 21 hour rules'.

Measuring Careers Service activities

Other local factors may also affect inter-authority comparability. For example, in predominantly rural LEAs a problem of a relative paucity of YTS places may be compounded by an aversion of young people to move to other parts of the country to attend YTS programmes. Such a move can be a difficult step for a 16 year old, and it is hard to see how a Careers Service could be held responsible if there is resistance to such suggestions.

As might be expected, the cumulative effect of these numerous limitations may severely limit the usefulness of these indicators at the inter-authority level. In particular, given the relative expense of outreach work with the young unemployed, and pressures on PCOs to perform well in delivering other services (common YTS application systems, for example), careful consideration would need to be given to any performance measure which might 'force' PCOs into what they might see as an inefficient allocation of resources.

Finally, it must be recognised that there is a political dimension to these indicators which relates to moves to revoke benefit from young people not willing to attend a YTS programme without good reason. These arguments are further complicated by the situation of those attending college on the DHSS 12 or 21 hour rule. Until this debate is resolved caution is necessary in proposing any inter-authority indicators which put the Careers Service in the position of appearing to police benefit schemes, particularly if the indicators themselves present methodological problems. The risk of imposing inappropriate output measures is, in the least, perverse effects like a focus on quantity of placements at the expense of quality of guidance, and at worst a reduction of valuable CSB-LEA cooperation in data collection, and thus the quality of policy relevant information flows overall.

Supplementary input and activity measures
In Chapter 3 it was noted that where output measures were problematic or presented only a partial picture, it was sometimes useful to devise more modest schemes of appraisal which supplemented output measures with indicators of costs and provision of service. Although these are not output measures, they can provide useful background

Performance monitoring

information to management. The following measures have been considered for the Careers Service:

Input measures
- Cost of service per young person
- Staffing ratio
- Staff grading ratio
- Proportion of qualified Careers Officers

Activity measures
- Interview ratios
- School guidance interview coverage

The monitoring of average costs over time, for example staff costs per 15+ year olds in maintained schools', is clearly useful at the intra-authority level. Keeping track of such costs on an annual basis is something already done by many Careers Services. Conversely, for the reasons explained in Chapter 4, attempts to compare such information at the inter-authority level is probably futile because of the differing service needs, ranges of service coverage, and local responses in terms of political and financial priorities. Interpreting average cost information cannot be done without detailed local knowledge.

By the same token, staffing ratios (number of staff to number of 15+ school pupils) are of interest locally because they monitor both changes in staff numbers and changes in the client base over time. However, in the absence of standardised Careers Service tasks, and without local knowledge, such indicators say very little about the performance of different Careers Services. Similarly a staff grading ratio, which indicates numbers of Careers Officers to number of support staff, seems a reasonable measure at first glance, but is made complicated by the fact that Careers Service support staff, and particularly Employment Assistants, do much valuable work directly with clients. Except with local knowledge, there is no obvious way to assess an appropriate balance between the work and costs of different grades of staff. Indicators like the staff grading ratio have little meaning outside of their local context.

A similar indicator is 'the number of qualified Careers Officers as a proportion of total number of Careers Officers'. The reference here is to the fact that in the past, Careers Officers were accepted into the service without the formal qualification 'Diploma in Vocational Guidance' which is now available. Although the objective of gradually reducing the numbers of unqualified Careers Officers is valid, it is not possible to make the assumption that experienced staff without formal qualifications provide a service which is in any way inferior to that provided by staff with formal qualifications but less experience.

Finally there are two activity measures which are of considerable interest at the intra-authority level, but virtually meaningless at the inter-authority level. The first are interview ratios, for example, 'number of 15+ interviews to number of appropriate staff'. Similar ratios can be developed for post-school guidance, FE guidance etc. Monitoring this activity at the intra-authority level over time gives a feel for any changes in the relative importance of the interview among the array of Careers Service functions, given changes in the client base. Similarly, a 'school guidance interview coverage ratio' relates the number of school guidance interviews to the number of 15+ pupils in any year. Monitoring this over time can help alert Careers Services as to the results of policy alterations or to *de facto* changes in practice. However the degree of coverage itself is a function of local professional priorities and available resources, and while it may be interesting to be aware of differing practices, it conveys no information on performance *per se*.

Conclusion

It has been argued that performance monitoring systems should be simple, cost-effective, involve reliable data easy to replicate on a systematic basis, and designed to encourage good performance.

A number of measures have been identified which might prove useful at the intra-authority level, that is for the purpose of an individual Careers Service monitoring its resource level, client base, and patterns of service delivery over time. However because of the complexity of the service described in earlier chapters, there appears to be no quantitative indicator or group of indicators which can measure overall performance, nor performance of the main tasks. What is possible is to build up a recurring picture of parts of the service to assist in management decision making.

Performance monitoring

In terms of inter-authority monitoring, some of the methodological problems identified here might be overcome with diligent longer-term research and intensive data analysis, but others will not. The question must be asked whether, in view of the number of difficulties, it is cost effective to continue to attempt to devise inter-authority output and performance indicators for the Careers Service. It may not be, and better system performance might come from improved professional inspection combined with an enhanced management information system which extends the input and throughput measures of the CSMR to what might be argued are genuine output measures, that is destinations of young people.

6 The Inspectorate: A Professional Mode of Performance Assessment

Introduction
Although intra-authority performance assessment is an important local management function there is much to be said for the independent assessment of local Careers Service activities, such as is already carried out by the Inspectorate of the Careers Service Branch.

The National Consumer Council (1986, p.6.18) also turned to the option of professional inspection as a means of performance assessment when it failed to generate any performance indicators in its study of day care/educational provision:

> Quality assessment must remain a matter of judgement. One of the best examples of professional judgement in the education service is provided by the reports on schools and local authorities prepared by members of HM Inspectorate. If HMIs base their judgements on any formal criteria, these are not generally made known and it seems likely that experience plays a major part.

A review of the Audit Commission's (1986) recommendations on performance assessment in education also reveals considerable reliance on the skills and services of H.M. Inspectors for Education. This not surprising because:

Performance monitoring

- inspectors are neutral, dispassionate and divorced from day-to-day operational considerations and local politics in a way in which no local authority employee can be; and
- inspectors are able to synthesize quantitative and qualitative information on performance and to assess this against a background knowledge of local operational constraints and work practices in other authorities.

Similarly, the recent appointment by the Training Commission of training standards inspectors within a Training Standards Advisory Service for YTS again suggests that reliance on an inspectorate is a generally promising option for performance assessment where there are multiple objectives and responses and where quantitative analysis faces methodological constraints.

The role of the Careers Service Inspectorate

The activities of the Careers Service Inspectorate are derived from the statutory obligations of Local Education Authorities 'to provide the Secretary of State, in such manner and at such times as he may specify, with such information and facilities for obtaining information as he may specify with respect to the performance' of their Careers Service functions. Since 1984 there has been provision for 13 Inspectors posts in England and one in Wales. The reports of the Inspectorate are technically a report to the Secretary of State, but are also passed back to the Local Education Authority as a detailed assessment of the service and how it might be improved.

Although this suggests that the Inspectorate serves different functions at different levels of government, there seems to be no great difficulty in reconciling these functions. This may be due to the generally constructive and helpful manner in which inspections are carried out. Careers Service Branch guidelines reflect this:

> For Careers Service managers and their staff an inspection provides an opportunity to review their activities in a critical (but supportive) framework. Inspectors seek to build on existing strengths, encouraging the development of plans and ideas within the service, but also challenge existing practices by suggesting more effective ways of operating. With growing

The inspectorate

pressure on the service in recent years increasing emphasis has been given to the need to decide priorities and more effective management to achieve them.

Again the CSB notes that 'An inspector is expected to become not only famliar with the organisation and systems, but also acquire an understanding of the problems facing the Service and ways in which these are being tackled'. Suggestions for improvement will have been previously discussed at length with LEA staff and managers so that when the inspection report appears it does not contain any unexpected ideas.

This constructive and interactive approach to performance appraisal which characterises the Careers Service Inspectorate no doubt accounts for the genuine enthusiasm for inspections which was expressed by a number of Principal Careers Officers. The extent to which a constructive approach is based on human relationships is also revealed in CSB documentation:

> The degree of success of fieldwork depends upon the relationship which an inspector can achieve with Careers Service staff at all levels. At best, there is sufficient trust on all sides to ensure a constructive outcome. Inspectors are then particularly conscious of the need to repay that trust by making all staff aware of their ideas and conclusions before reporting formally.

The inspection process

The scope of any particular inspection can vary according to the size and circumstances of the local Careers Service. In a small, geographically compact Careers Services the inspector will look at its work as a whole, from policy development through to the guidance work of individual careers officers. In a larger Careers Service with geographic sub-divisions, some inspections will focus on the whole range of the work of the service in a particular sub-division. These types of inspections will be interspersed with an inspection of the overall management and organisation of the Service, but without an evaluation of guidance work.

Performance monitoring

Generally during the course of an inspection the inspector will be addressing the following broad questions:
- Are policies clear and translated into practical plans?
- Do all staff know what is expected of them?
- Is the work (including guidance work) monitored?
- Are relationships with schools and colleges purposeful and meeting the individual needs of pupils/students?
- Is there an appropriate balance in the priority given to meeting the needs of various clients/ groups (pupils, students, employers, unemployed, trainees etc)?
- Are contacts with employers effective and an adequate record system in use?
- Is the system for reviewing the needs of unemployed young people and other special groups effective?

The detailed aspects of LEA activity which may be addressed, all or in part, in an inspection are set by Careers Service Branch as:

Background Information
- economic, social, administrative, and demographic such as 5th year school population, unemployment rates, YTS and placement rates.

Management and Organisation
- LEA setting and relationships. Committee responsibilities within the LEA.
- Policy formulation and dissemination procedures. Objectives and priorities as set out in policy documents.
- Organisational structure and staff responsibilities.
- Communications and consultation procedures.
- Operational plans and monitoring procedures.
- Deployment of staff, workloads, turnover.
- Qualifications of staff. Extent of management evaluation of guidance.
- Training needs assessment and in-service training.
- DE funded staff use.

The inspectorate

- Office network and adequacy of premises. Opening hours.
- Careers information and library facilities
- General effectiveness of management function.

Work in Educational Institutions
- LEA policy for careers education. Advisory functions. Careers Teacher training.
- Careers Service role in curriculum development and careers information.
- Policy and arrangements for careers officers' activities in schools.
- Evaluation of guidance.
- Summaries of guidance and records.

Employment work
- Organisation, planning and monitoring.
- Collecting, storing and retrieving information on employers.
- Contacts with employers/YTS providers and marketing of Service.
- Procedures for recording and filling vacancies.
- Services to YTS providers and trainers.
- Extent of attention to needs of unemployed young people.
- Extent of attention to needs (including guidance) of trainees/employees.
- Review of equal opportunities issues.
- Effectiveness of employment work.

It is recognised by CSB that inspections may be used by PCOs quite legitimately to promote policies and actions which, in the view of the PCO, have not been given sufficient priority within the LEA. In the past additional staff or better premises were the main concern but now concern is more likely to involve the development of new Careers Service functions. CSB appropriately recommends that 'an inspector needs to take a balanced view of such ideas and appreciate the pressures which exist within the Authority'.

Strengthening the Inspectorate to enhance performance appraisal functions

For all the general goodwill about the inspectorate there are concerns which may need to be addressed if it is to further the interests of performance appraisal within the Careers Service. These points will not be revelations to CSB or the Inspectorate, and in the main they arise from comments made by PCOs in discussion with the researcher.

First, inspections do not always occur with sufficient frequency. Major developments and reorganisations within local Careers Services may go unexamined for some years even, as was suggested, when PCOs request an inspection. The reason PCOs would make such a request is that they view the Inspectorate as a kind of in-house management consulting service to which they would hope to turn for review and advice on organisational change and administrative initiatives. That PCOs do view the Inspectorate in this fashion is wholly positive and demonstrates an evolving organisational culture, of the type recommended by the Audit Commission, in which performance appraisal is seen as a useful and challenging management function. However, within the Careers Service Branch, there may be insufficient inspectors' positions for the task required of the Inspectorate. This can present a difficulty because a balance of increased expenditure may be necessary to take full advantage of the benefits of performance assessment by an adequately staffed, trained and experienced Inspectorate. Here, as in many cases, the trade off between economy and service effectiveness is a matter for the reasoned judgment of management.

Second, there is concern about a lack of experience of actual Careers Service work on the part of inspectors, particularly when compared with the PCOs whom they are advising. One might expect a number of inspectors to be retired PCOs but low administative grading for inspectors' positions generally precludes this situation. The CSB programme to promote APCO and Careers Officer secondments for three to four years to the Inspectorate may ameliorate this situation, although, from a performance appraisal point of view, the relative lack of administrative stature of the inspectors' positions may mean that very qualified people like PCOs are still not attracted to the posts. Similarly the relative stature of CSB vis-a-vis the LEAs may be somewhat restrained by the relatively low grading of the posts.

On the other hand, the CSB puts considerable effort into training and support for inspectors. One example is the Vocational Guidance Interview Checklist package (Bedford, 1982) which sets out a model of good practice in vocational guidance interviews based on a large scale survey of guidance interviews in schools. From this a checklist is proposed by which inspectors sitting in on interviews can assess changes in student attitudes with regard to focus on options, degree of knowledge of preferred options and the range of available options, realism in relation to abilities and the labour market, and the extent to which students have worked out practical steps to achieve career objectives. Inspectors undergo a training programme in using the checklist, and in developing their own reliability in assessing interviews.

A third point is that the lack of advancement opportunities for inspectors has resulted in considerable turnover. As many as four to six of the 14 inspectors' posts have been vacant at any one time. This has resulted not only in a reduction of the numbers of inspections carried out, but in the loss of inspector expertise in evaluation, for example of the quality of guidance interviews, which is developed at considerable expense by Careers Service Branch. In general, the more experienced an inspector, both in Careers Service work and in inspection, the more adequate the critique and the more useful the recommendations that might be made. The National Consumer Council (1986, p.6.18) takes a similar view in their suggestion that experience is a major factor in determining judgement criteria by HM Inspectorate for Education. The situation of high turnover in the Careers Service Inspectorate may not be cost effective in the longer term.

Finally, in addition to the inspection of individual services, there may be an increased role for the Inspectorate in the study of common themes and problems, and in the dissemination of good practice which can enhance performance across the entire Careers Service. For example, the Inspectorate might study a single functional area of service (say, work experience coordination, computerisation of management information, or guidance services to high flyers) over a range of LEAs

Performance monitoring

and draw conclusions on meeting common problems and innovative solutions. This information would be of interest to all Careers Services. The Inspectorate might also wish to develop further its knowledge of ways of developing strategic management skills to assist local Careers Services to cope with organisational change, and to promote performance through better management practices.

7 Enhancing Performance Through the Careers Service Management Information System

Introduction
The Careers Service information system works at two levels. The first level consists of joint information gathering and synthesis between LEAs and the Careers Service Branch. In this case the Careers Service Management Return (CSMR, Appendix D) is used by LEAs to transmit information on their activities and clients to CSB, which collates and analyses that data on an LEA, regional and national basis. The second level consists of additional information bases developed by local Careers Services for their own policy making and management purposes, sometimes with assistance from CSB in terms of the development of computer and software capacity. The purpose of this and the subsequent chapter is to review briefly the relevance of the existing information system for performance appraisal, and to make suggestions for further interaction between local Careers Services and CSB to provide an additional flow of information on client destinations.

Destination statistics in the information system
At least part of the usefulness of these recommendations might arise from CSB monitoring of issues which have wide policy implications,

and in CSB developing further its strategic guidance and monitoring role to local authorities. In a decentalised system like the Careers Service, which nevertheless addresses many issues of national concern in a context of rapid socioeconomic change and considerable regional diversity, the importance of strategic guidance and intelligence to system performance is not to be underestimated.

The review of the potential for performance indicators in Chapter 4 suggested that few realistic quantitative indicators of genuine performance are likely to become available, as opposed to existing measures of system inputs or activities. These are well covered by the CSMR. However, one fact which was apparent from the fieldwork was the importance of school leaver and other destination statistics to policy discussions about the role of the Careers Services generally, about its influence with clients, and the balance between destinational options and choices in various LEAs. This view was reinforced by the observation that many Careers Services already collect good destination statistics because they themselves find it useful for their policy making and information purposes. In the most sophisticated systems the information is collected for statutory school leavers, lower and upper sixth formers, YTS leavers, and FE leavers, disaggregated by such factors as sex, ethnic origin, education speciality (TVEI, CPVE) and occupational category in training or employment as appropriate.

Following from this, the proposition set out in this chapter is simple - that each Careers Service might collect standardised annual destination statistics in the same month and that the coordination of the data collection exercise could be undertaken by CSB. This approach has the benefits of being simple, cost effective and relevant to policy needs at both LEA and CSB levels. At the local level it would give PCOs and Careers Service staff information on young peoples' destinations in their local authority compared to other LEAs, and trend data from year to year. LEAs could be grouped for comparison purposes. At an aggregated level it would provide CSB with a management tool useful in discussions with DES, the Training Commission and other agencies. At a national level, the numerous requests in parliamentary questions for this kind of information indicates its relevance to policy debates. At any level destination statistics provide information on the context and

Enhacing performance through the Careers Service

results of Careers Service activity and careers education, information on new and developing service needs, essential background to policy discussions of elected members; and information on staying-on rates into full-time education, youth employment rates, and entry rates to YTS and its relative importance compared with traditional destinations. The material also helps in discussions with MSC about whether more YTS places need to be created and in which occupational categories, and in planning in the Non-Advanced Further Education (NAFE) sector.

One apparent advantage of this proposal is that it conforms with accepted views that where outcome measurement is difficult or impossible, the development of increased management information flows is a useful way to proceed. Further, while the appropriateness of any aspect of the information as a measure of system performance is open to discussion, the usefulness of these statistics does not hinge on that point. On the contrary their usefulness as statistical background to current policy debates and as a pre-requisite for good management stands whatever their relevance as a performance measure. Destination statistics represent a conjunction of the Careers Service's intelligence and service functions and their absence may diminish performance.

Rather than focus limited CSB statistical resources on the methodologically difficult tasks of trying to devise placement indicators, it may be more profitable to extend from CSMR to the enhancement of policy relevant information in the form of destination statistics. These destination statistics although not directly indicative of performance, are fundamental to any understanding of the context and the results of vocational transition and guidance and are therefore an essential increment of managment information. Further the Careers Service is in the unique position of having this information available, through the local Careers Services, on a virtual census, as opposed to sample, basis for the entire country. This information could begin to be available within about eight months of the July leaving date for statutory leavers.

At the national level the collection of destination statistics is in keeping with joint DES/DE/Welsh Office initiatives in promoting careers

Performance monitoring

education and guidance, as set out in *Working Together for a Better Future* (1987):

> The Careers Service should also be involved with schools and colleges in monitoring the progress of pupils during their transitional years, and if possible, subsequently: this sort of information can be vital to schools and colleges in monitoring their own performance in preparing and guiding their pupils and students.

Destination statistics are required as answers for numerous parliamentary questions, many of which can now only be answered in part, thus losing the benefits of an holistic overview of the conjunction of education and employment. At both national and regional levels destination statistics address fundamental issues about the transition from school to work, and about the differential penetration and importance of new initiatives like YTS, CPVE, or TVEI, compared with traditional if diminishing arrangements for employment and training. For example, destination statistics provide a useful overview of regional variation in staying-on rates, and the issue of access to and take-up of opportunities in further and higher education is near the top of the political agenda in areas where traditional sources of 16+ employment have all but disappeared. The same is true wherever the introduction of tertiary colleges is planned, a development which often pushes up participation rates.

Destination statistics also can illuminate local, regional and national changes engendered by new initiatives like two year YTS, and can help consideration about questions such as the trade-off between YTS attendance and sixth form or full-time further education, possible discriminatory effects of YTS age limits in terms of ethnic origin, or the implications of the local relationship between YTS and CPVE or TVEI take-up. There are many other examples which can be given but the main point may be that management of the Careers Service in the absence of destination statistics could be less effective either when socio-demographic circumstances are changing or when new initiatives like YTS dramatically alter the flows of young people among destinations. A number of PCOs, for example, expressed the view that

Enhacing performance through the Careers Service

they simply could not 'manage' without destination statistics. PCOs made these points:

> How can any Careers Service make reasonable decisions without destination statistics? Destination statistics are essential for thinking about both the results of last years' guidance and the task for the coming year ... They help reduce common misconceptions about the working of the local labour market, for example, that young people do not find employment after YTS ... They lend realism to guidance, for example if 200 young people want to go on nursery nursing courses and we know that only a small percentage of last year's students ended up working as nursery nurses ... Destination statistics are essential for education authority policy-making.

More specifically, the case for systematic collection of destination statistics includes the following points:
- Destination statistics are illuminative of broad trends and regional variations at the conjunction of statutory education, FHE, training and employment.
- Destination statistics can help to impart realism not only to policy discussions, but to the guidance process itself, insofar as they tell us about the actual experience of young people, as opposed to common 'myths' about what goes on. The information can be used nationally at the LEA level, and by individual careers officers in the interview.
- Destination statistics are essential for providing feedback to careers educators in schools, for planning of work-related non-advanced further education, for planning YTS programmes, and for monitoring equal opportunities policies.
- Destination statistics are a powerful source of information and, to the extent that knowledge is power, their availability can raise the stature of the Careers Service at all levels. This may be useful in inter-agency discussion at all levels of government.

Of course many PCOs already realise the importance of destination statistics in management, in developing their strategic intelligence function, and thus in raising the stature of the Careers Service within

Performance monitoring

the LEA. Similar arguments may apply to the possible national collection of destination statistics.

Local authority capacity in surveying destinations
The capacity of local Careers Services to survey destinations varies considerably. Of the 12 Careers Services studied in this project, ten collected destination statistics. Of the two which did not, one planned to do so in the near future. However one PCO was of the opinion that destination statistics were unnecessary. A programme to further develop this type of statistical capability would need to begin with a full survey of existing capabilities of all local authorities and their plans for the future. However, from the small sample described here a number of points are of interest.

First, in 11 of the 12 cases there was considerable enthusiasm on the part of PCOs, APCOs and other staff both for the usefulness *and* further potential of destination statistics. All 11 PCOs saw their destination statistics as central to the development of a policy-related information system, and all had planned developments in hand. Those whose statistical systems were already computerised looked forward to further refinement of the interactive capabilities of the system and development of software. Those whose systems were not computerised planned computerisation, usually within the next year or two. Most Careers Services either collected data for up to four or five groups of leavers (statutory school leavers, lower and upper sixth formers, FE attenders, and YTS leavers) or looked forward to the day when they might do so. A few collected further data on HE leavers or on the unemployed. But statistical capacity varied considerably according to local priorities and resource constraints. Any enhancement programme would need to be developmental, phased over time, and offer positive encouragement to local authorities to make further investments in their statistical systems. In particular there is considerable potential and enthusiasm for inter-authority learning which could be fostered by CSB in a programme similar to the recently completed DEMACS programme (DE Microcomputer Assistance for the Careers Service).

Second, all of this group collected destination statistics for statutory school leavers in similar fashion, which was on a full census rather than a sampling basis. This obviates many sampling problems and provides a more complete and sustainable picture. The collection of information is part of a rolling programme which begins in July and with a termination date dictated by local needs. As a first step in this process either school or Careers Service surveys all school leavers by questionnaire (sample in Appendix E), with a follow-up reminder, and then telephone follow-ups take place as necessary until the cut-off date. On the whole the picture is of *first* destinations. The biggest group of careers services have cut-off dates between the end of September and mid-October, with a second group opting for a late November or early December cut-off. A single service of the eleven opted for a mid-January date. Again a survey of Careers Services would show the overall pattern.

Third, response rates to destination surveys varied considerably from one authority to the next. The best Careers Services were able to reduce the non-response rate for statutory leavers to as low as 3 per cent, and these tended to be counties with a large rural population and smaller, non-metropolitan urban areas. Conversely, surveys in large metropolitan counties or on the fringes of big cities had non-response rates as high as about 13 per cent. Particular problems were evident where populations were relatively mobile, and/or where there were high numbers of immigrant families or families of ethnic minority origin, for many of whom English was not a first language. A compounding factor was a relatively low incidence of household telephones in some inner city areas. In local authorities with these characteristics propensity to respond to a questionnaire or a telephone survey was naturally lower than elsewhere.

In terms of reduction of non-response rates, PCOs argued that a) it was not cost-effective for them to allocate additional resources to attempt to reduce the non-response rate further, and b) in any event the amount of information generated was sufficient for their policy making and management purposes. Overall, something in the order of a 90 per cent response rate could be expected nationally for statutory leaver destinations. This rate would probably improve as further experience in information collection was gained by local Careers Services. In fact, given that what takes place is a national census rather than a survey, the

Performance monitoring

response rate is very credible and sufficient as well for national purposes, especially as this is a monitoring rather than an evaluation exercise.

Fourth, all eleven of the PCOs in authorities collecting statistics expressed a willingness to cooperate with CSB in assembling national level destination statistics. They saw this as a natural extension of CSMR and the DEMACs developments. However, each stressed that the enhancement of statistical capacity would need to be phased in over 2-3 years, and that when the programme is in operation quick and regular feedback of national, regional, and 'similar authority' information from CSB to local Careers Services was essential to ensure continued cooperation. PCOs perceived that strengthening the hand of the Careers Service at the national level might be to their benefit in local political negotiations.

Other sources of destination statistics

While there are other sources of destination statistics none quite replicates the potential of a Careers Service system as they either have a different client focus (e.g. graduates) or they are not designed so much as permanent recurring monitoring programmes but as one off in-depth research projects. The information system proposed here complements rather than duplicates any existing systems.

Some destination statistics will be made available from the England and Wales Youth Cohort (Pathways) sample over the next two years. However the Pathways project, which will provide a large amount of data useful for further analysis based on a lengthy questionnaire, will be completed about 1989, about the time when a Careers Service system might get off the ground. The Pathways project, because it is research-based, has been devised on considerably different terms from that envisaged here.

More relevant to this proposal is the First Destinations Survey of Graduates (FDS) conducted by universities, polytechnics, and other institutes of higher education. This provides a useful model for this work. The survey is carried annually by all universities' Careers Services in the UK on behalf of the Universities' Statistical Record (USR, 1986) for the University Grants Committee; by the Association

Enhacing performance through the Careers Service

of Graduate Careers Advisory Service (AGCAS, 1986) for all polytechnics; and by the Association of Careers Advisors in Colleges of Higher Education (ACACHE, 1986) for most students qualifying from full-time and sandwich courses in Colleges and Institutes of Higher Education.

The FDS data collection process is described by Tarsh (1987) on behalf of DES, which processes the college and polytechnic information on behalf of AGCAS and ACACHE. Each Careers Service sends out a short postal questionnaire (sample, Appendix F) asking new graduates to supply information on their first firm destination after graduation. Non-respondents and unemployed graduates receive follow-up questionnaires up to the end of the calendar year of departure from college or university. The response rate to the postal survey is in the order of 60-70 per cent of graduates. The response rate is then improved by follow-up contact between careers officers and respondents, course tutors, parents, friends and other sources. The final response rate is about 90 per cent for colleges and universities and about 80 per cent for polytechnics. Results are collated into national totals for each of the three sectors, and published about one year after graduation, or in the middle of the subsequent calendar year. Aside from the simple destinational categories (employment, unemployment, further study or training, not available for employment, leaving country), those graduates who enter employment are also asked for their occupation and sector of employment. This information is coded in great detail for further analysis, although published figures use summary classifications, divided by sex.

Appendix G gives example of tables generated by FDS, which is similar in both data collection procedure and output to that proposed here. This survey has been carried for over ten years and the useful body of data enables broad trends to be discussed by commentators, for example:

> Two broad trends may be seen: the growing participation of women, and the expansion of polytechnics and colleges of higher education relative to universities, particularly between 1983 and 1985. In the labour market, teacher training and public service employment have given way to financial and commercial services. Overall, prospects for graduate

employment have improved from their all-time low in 1982 (Tarsh, 1987).

The FDS, it must be stressed is a *first* destination survey, just as that proposed here, and this does have some limitations. In particular, there is currently debate over the use of FDS to generate 'Unemployment and Degree Subject' tables (in Appendix G) which can be interpreted to read that graduates with arts subjects degrees may have a more difficult time securing permanent employment. In rather intense debate, other researchers (e.g. Kelly et al., 1986; Brennan et al., 1987) counter that this is a temporary phenomenon and that the lack of a career path dimension in the FDS paints a distorted and unfair picture.

It is not the intention here to comment on the debate, but it does point out that monitoring efforts are not a substitute for in-depth research projects and that constraints imposed on a monitoring programme (tight resource effectiveness, fast turn-around of information, etc.) can always result in debate about the quality of the data, particularly if the information is relevant to on-going political discussions. Monitoring efforts are not meant to supplant dedicated research but to paint a useful, recurring picture on a regular basis.

Conclusions

1. There is a strong case for enhancement of the Careers Service management information system by supplementing the input and activity information generated by the Careers Service Management Return (CSMR) with further policy relevant information in the form of national destination statistics. It has been argued that destination statistics are of such importance to policy discussions that they should be collected on an annual recurring basis rather than in one-off research projects, as they are now. The Careers Service has the capacity to implement this important part of a management information system.

2. It may be that as far as inter-authority data is concerned it is not cost- effective to continue to attempt to develop intermediate output measures, in the form of placing activities in employment and in YTS. Such information is already available and useful to local Careers Services from CSMR but aggregation above that level of

analysis may present more problems than can be resolved efficiently.
3. A national destination survey of statutory school leavers touches on only one part of Careers Service work, and might profitably be supplemented by other destination survey material, for example, of YTS leavers, lower and upper sixth form leavers, and FE leavers, as appropriate. Even then it says nothing about 19+ clients of the Careers Service.
4. Local Careers Services are each at a different stage in the development and computerisation of destination statistics and a developmental programme spread over about three years would be necessary. The next chapter outlines such a programme.

8 Enhancing Capacity in Monitoring Young People's Destinations

Introduction
To undertake regular destination analysis on a national basis would require a degree of standardisation which would allow inter-authority comparability. For this it would be necessary to have:
- standardised definitions of destination categories;
- an agreed date for the survey to take place;
- standard categories for disaggregation;
- the commitment of all LEAs to carrying out the survey;
- in-house capacity within CSB to analyse and redistribute the data; and
- a development programme.

A development programme for destination statistics
A development programme for destination statistics might consist of the following steps:
1. Survey of existing practice and plans of the 104 Careers Services in England and Wales.
2. Preparation of guidelines for standardised definitions and categories, and a suggested schedule for developing capacity to survey Statutory Leavers, YTS Leavers, Lower 6th Leavers, Upper

6th Leavers and FE Leavers, disaggregated by sex, ethnic origin and occupational or training category.
3. Consideration of software requirements and the means for dissemination of good practice and advice on computerisation.
4. Consideration of resource implications of programme and possible contractual arrangements between CSB and local Careers Services.
5. Pilot of national destination survey.

The first step in the development of a programme would be to mount a survey of the statistical capabilities and the plans of all 104 Careers Services in England and Wales, posing the following main questions to Principal Careers Officers and statistical officers:
- To what extent do you collect destination statistics and what are your plans in this regard?
- For what categories of leavers do you survey destinations and by what factors are these disaggregated?
- For what purposes do you collect destination statistics?
- What is the process and the schedule by which this information is collected?
- What is your cut-off date in data collection?
- Is the survey on a sample basis or on a census basis?
- Is your record keeping system computerised and what are your plans for computerisation?
- Is your focus on first destination after leaving or existing destination at time of survey?
- Do you note ethnic origin, occupational category or other types of information where appropriate?
- What further assistance do you require in developing your capability to monitor destinations?

At the same time as the questionnaire is being circulated, existing publications of local authority destinations statistics can be analysed for similarities and differences in approach. These are almost always annual publications prepared by Careers Services in autumn or early spring, either dealing specifically with destinations or as part of an annual report on that Careers Service.

Performance monitoring

Following the survey a practical plan for developing a minimum level of capability in all Careers Services could be worked out, with phased stages of development, for example from a survey of statutory school leavers, to the upper-sixth form, lower sixth form, and on to YTS or FE leavers. It would be very useful at this stage to develop a model standardised system, which would suggest a minimum level of development at the end of each year of the programme.

As noted, local authorities are at very different stages in statistical development in this area, and differing resource constraints and political priorities are in operation. However, there appears to be widespread enthusiasm for the usefulness of destination statistics among many PCOs and local elected members of education authorities. This appreciation could be useful in promoting further development. Elected members may find that they *wish* to have this information and view developments and costs in this area on a positive basis. Dissemination of information on the overall programme to all elected education authority members in England and Wales, via PCOs, may be helpful.

A development programme would need to set out a timetable which encourages progress, but does not impose overly arduous demands on Careers Services which are only beginning to develop their statistical capacity. As a general rule the programme which will have the most chance of success is one which accords closely with existing and planned statistical developments in local authorities, meets CSB's minimum data requirements, and imposes least costs on local authorities and CSB. It may be that statistical sophistication or broadness of data collection objectives will need to be compromised by organisational or resource constraints. However, these are pragmatic decisions and once again full knowledge of the existing situation in all Careers Services is a prerequisite for setting out the detailed development programme.

Without a more full understanding of the organisational constraints in operation it would be presumptuous to set out a model for destination statistics at this time. However it is possible to look at existing good practice in the ten surveyed authorities and to make certain suggestions. First, a number of PCOs expressed the view that the most sophisticated

Enhancing capacity in monitoring young people

statistical system was that of the City of Birmingham Careers Service. This is being adopted as a model by other Careers Services, at least in part. That system is described below. Second, a probable best time for the cut-off of data collection and transmission to CSB for a statutory leavers survey is suggested. Third, a number of categories for disaggregation of data are discussed.

An example of use of destination statistics

Appendix H provides selected samples of output of destination statistics from a number of local authorities. These are included to give an overview of the use of the statistics by some local authorities. These are far from the complete set of output for any one local authority, some of which are now very substantial and may run to 35 pages of analysis and more. Of the ten Careers Services reviewed here, the City of Birmingham appears to have the most advanced information system, and other local authorities are considering acquiring some of their software. It is worth reviewing the Birmingham system briefly to show possible areas for statistical system development around a nucleus of destination statistics.

The Birmingham system is known as the 'Young Persons Record System' (YPRS) and consists of three linked files. The YPRS file contains data on each statutory school leaver in the Birmingham state education system: name, date of birth, ethnic origin, subjects taken, exam results, goals at 16, work experience, guidance given, and 16+ destination. This information is updated as necessary at 17, 18 and 19 years of age. The second file is called the Opportunities File and lists all available placements in YTS and in employment. These are sent out daily for display at Birmingham's six Careers Centres and to neighbouring Careers Services. The third file is the Employers Register, which records type of firm, number of employees, and skill levels in the workforce, for all firms which have placed young people or offered placements or work experience.

Inter-file linkages in the YPRS are as follows. There is an interactive facility between the YPRS file and the Opportunities File which automatically scans and searches overnight for possible matches between placement opportunities and young people registered in YPRS.

Performance monitoring

Second, the Employers Register contains YPRS file information on individual young people placed in local firms, and this is updated as new information becomes available. It also enables Careers Officers to inquire as to the status and success of past placements. Additionally when there is no match between a young person registered in YPRS and available opportunities, the Employers Register can be scanned for possible employers who might have vacancies and these can be contacted to determine if any vacancies are likely or if YTS placements can be arranged.

This information generated by YPRS does not remain within the Careers Service alone but is transmitted elsewhere in the local authority. Destination data automatically go back to the schools, and when combined with occupational training or placement information, and subject to geographic breakdown, to the college division of the education authority for training and work-related NAFE planning, and to MSC for YTS planning. Destination information disaggregated by sex and race is sent to the Equal Opportunities Unit. An updated Employers Register is regularly sent to the Birmingham Economic Development Office. These activities are seen as consolidating the Careers Service's intelligence function within the local authority.

Developments planned for the Birmingham system include an eventual extension of YPRS files on individuals back to 13, 14, and 15 years of age to record details of option choice work and group guidance work at these ages. YPRS records may be opened on adults as well, which would enable a 'reverse tracking' of career paths to be undertaken. The Opportunities File may be extended to include educational opportunities in and out of Birmingham. It is hoped that the Employers Register will eventually cover all employers in Birmingham rather than only those in contact with the Careers Service. Finally the City of Birmingham is currently decentralising services to about 40 planned neighbourhood offices and opportunities information will be transmitted daily to those offices for display.

Timing of the statutory leavers' survey

In terms of suggested month of the statutory school leavers survey two factors need to be considered. First, whatever is proposed should accommodate as nearly as is possible existing practice in Careers Services. Second, there are local variations in labour market operation which need to be considered. The majority (six) of Careers Services of the ten surveyed imposed a cut-off point at the end of September or in early October. These dates were found to be most useful in terms of preparing documentation on the previous school year for Annual Reports for elected members, for purposes of reporting to committees, and for giving feedback to schools. However a significant minority (i.e. three) found it better to set the cut-off in late November or the first week in December, and this minority includes ILEA, at present the largest Careers Service in the country.

Late autumn closing dates for a statutory leavers' survey are chosen for a number of good reasons having to do with local labour market operation. First, in areas of relatively low unemployment, like Greater London or the Southeast, school leavers may feel with some justification that temporary unemployment in early autumn, while they are actively scanning the possibilities for employment, is preferable to a YTS placement. By the end of November this situation is said to have diminished and school leavers usually have sorted out their preferred option, thus giving a truer picture of first destination. Second, in areas with a substantial amount of seasonal employment in tourism (the Devon Coast for example) many young people take temporary employment, after leaving school, which is nevertheless not a true first destination. Once again by late autumn this influence has ceased. Finally, any cut-off later, say in spring, tends to suffer from a fall off in response rate, and definitional problems over which destination, first or subsequent, was to be the focus of the study.

Pending a survey, it would seem that an appropriate cut-off for a national destination survey would be in early December. This date has the following advantages. It would appear to accommodate the majority of local Careers Services which impose either September/October or November/December cut-offs, without imposing unwelcome additional statistical burdens and additional, unwelcome expense. Most local authorities indicated that they would not have resources for more than one survey per client group per year. As the focus would be true first destinations there would be a

Performance monitoring

consistency of definitions across LEAs. A number of PCOs made the point that if a cut-off was in early December this would accord with the only 'slack' period for Careers staff between September and the following July, in which staff were relatively unburdened by guidance responsibilities. It was in December that PCOs felt that they could assign staff to collate and check data, which could then be sent to CSB in, say, the first week of January.

Categories for destination analysis

Whatever the working arrangements of local authorities, the only requirement for a national survey in terms of destination categories would be guidelines for defining categories and the ability of local authorities' categories or sub-categories to collapse into those suggested by CSB. The best way to do this would be to work from the full survey of local authority capacity. In the meantime, the following list is suggested from a review of the ten sets of statistics studied here:

A. 5TH YEAR SCHOOL LEAVERS SURVEY

   Stayed in Education
   - continued in 6th form (academic, CPVE, TVEI, GCSE resit)
   - attending 6th form college (as above)
   - attending further education college (as above)

   Entered Employment

   Entered YTS

   Unemployed

   Moved

   Unknown

B. SIXTH FORM SCHOOL LEAVERS (possible subcategories CPVE, TVEI, Lower, Upper, A level, AS level, GCSE resit)

   Attending Higher Education

   Attending Further Education

   Entered Employment

   Entered JTS

   Unemployed

Moved

Unknown

C. YOUNG PEOPLE LEAVING YTS

In Employment (Full or Part Time)
- with same employer
- with different employer

Returning to full time education

To another YTS programme

Unemployed

Moved

Unknown

D. FURTHER EDUCATION LEAVERS

Stayed in Education
- continued in FE
- in higher education

Entered Employment

Entered YTS

Unemployed

Moved

Unknown

Disaggregation by relevant variables

The need to disaggregate information by sex is obvious. More contentious is the question of disaggregation by ethnic origin, although the arguments for doing so are persuasive. The Commission for Racial Equality (1987) notes:

> The Careers Service is a major channel for young people joining the YTS scheme and therefore has a key role to play in ensuring that equal opportunities are provided.

Ethnic record keeping can:
- help demonstrate an authority's commitment to equal opportunity;

Performance monitoring

- help gain the confidence of minority communities through better understanding of their situation;
- provide an example for employers in the area;
- provide the data on which to judge the effectiveness of equal opportunities policies over time; and
- provide a factual basis for discussion of the ethnic aspects of recruitment and other employment policies, the differential effects of 'staying-on' or going on YTS, and other issues.

A number of Careers Services already collect statistics on ethnic origin, but obviously interest is considerably greater where there are substantial numbers of persons of non-white ethnic origin. However, whatever the local level of interest, if destination statistics are to have national impact every Careers Service must be willing to keep ethnic records. This may present problems insofar as whether to keep ethnic records is a rather contentious issue which leads to wide differences of opinion.

In terms of collapsable categories there are also problems. The Labour Force Survey asks people to respond to the question 'to which of these groups (listed on a card) do you consider you belong?' The card contains the following list:

> White, West Indian or Guyanese, Indian, Pakistani, Bangladeshi, Chinese, African, Arab, Mixed Origin, Other.

Analysis of the Labour Force Survey (Employment Gazette, January, 1987) groups 'Indian, Pakistani and Bangladeshi' as Asian, although that is a rather confusing term. However, using this type of complex list does require self-categorisation by respondents, and a firm and public commitment to ethnic record keeping. Some Careers Services skirt around the contentious aspects of ethnic record keeping by allowing Careers Officers to make visual assessments of ethnic origin, presumably without the clients being aware of the process. Where this is the case only very simple categories are possible: White, Afro-Caribbean (including African), Indian Sub-Continent and Other. A related problem is that in local authorities which do collect information on ethnic origin there is wide disparity in definitions. The term 'Afro-Caribbean' is taken by some to mean West Indian, Guyanese *and* African. In others 'Afro-Caribbean' means from the Caribbean and not African. It is not possible to suggest hard and fast categories without some study and careful consideration. Whatever is suggested will be judged disagreeable or wrong by some people. The general criteria are that categories must be relevant to policy, clearly distinguishable, and able to contain and allow local variation in sub-categories.

Equally problematic will be to agree on a set of occupational categories by which training and employment placements can be analysed. A review of the ten LEA data sets reveals only that no two groups of categories were the same, and that the number of categories ranges from nine to 34, depending perhaps on local needs. An appropriate set of ten to fifteen categories will need to be devised which will find general agreement among local Careers Services. Once again the topic is of such complexity and contention that an overview of existing practice and specialist advice is indicated.

Other issues
One further issue which may need attention, and which may become more pronounced, is the extent to which information on students in private or other independent or 'opted-out' schools would be included in the destination statistics. This is particularly an issue in counties like Surrey and others, where as much as 25 per cent of the student population may be in independent education.

A second question to be resolved is how exactly to classify unemployed leavers collecting benefit, who are attending college on the '21 hour rule'.

9 Conclusion

One obvious point is that genuine monitoring of performance in a professional public service, as opposed to increasing budgetary control, requires the systematic specification of the relationship of the inputs of a service to the outcomes. This has only been accomplished for public services where manual tasks are under review, or where tight control over service inputs and intervening variables can be combined with obvious positive or negative outcomes, for example, for some in-patient hospital services. Even if it was accepted that the guidance and placement needs of young people and the extent of the influence of Careers Services were measurable, there is ample evidence that the measurement task could not be done within reasonable constraints for efficient performance monitoring systems in government. A second point is that monitoring systems designed for the purposes of professional development and constructive staff feedback are not generally suitable for assessment of system performance, and vice-versa.

Local authority Careers Services, being unable to demonstrate the absolute benefits of their service delivery, and in response to circumstance, have been broadening the range of their activities within local authorities to include what I have called service coordination and policy intelligence functions. These include coordination of work experience programmes and Youth Training Scheme (YTS) application procedures, and preparation of sophisticated, computerised destination statistics covering statutory school leavers, sixth form leavers, YTS

Conclusion

leavers and further education leavers. These developments enhance local performance and the stature of Careers Services.

Conclusions on performance measurement
The most intractable problem in systematic monitoring of effectiveness of careers guidance lies in determining measurable objectives and the most useful criteria upon which to base judgements of effectiveness. In any attempt to measure the outcome of vocational guidance, it is difficult to control for external factors and the complex influence network which operates on vocational maturity. There may be no methodological resolution to these problems.

This report suggests that, for inter-local authority performance appraisal, neither approaches making use of client satisfaction measures or of quantitative performance indicators are likely to result in the development of a cost effective performance monitoring system. For reasons discussed at length in Chapters three and four, further efforts in this regard may continue to be unproductive, at least without substantial expenditure on dedicated research tasks as opposed to regular, resource-efficient monitoring activities. However, many Careers Services would like to do more in the way of performance appraisal and the assessment of client satisfaction, and a number already do good work in this regard. The report also examined practical ways to monitor Careers Service activities and to enhance intra-authority reviews of performance.

The Careers Service Inspectorate
The Careers Service Inspectorate, subject to certain limitations, already accords closely with the appreciative, contextual performance review system which this research suggests may be the most appropriate performance evaluation approach for the Careers Service. The report argued that the Inspectorate provides the most useful vehicle for both appraising individual local authority performance in the management and delivery of Careers Services, and for researching and encouraging good practice which can enhance performance of the system overall. Professional service systems in general can benefit from constructive, dispassionate inspection where output or performance measurement is unattainable.

Performance monitoring

The Careers Service management information system
A review of potential output or outcome indicators suggests that few realistic quantitative indicators of performance are likely to become available, as opposed to existing measures of system inputs or activities. These are already well covered by the Careers Service Management Return. One fact which was apparent from the fieldwork was the importance of school leaver and other destination statistics to policy discussions about the role of the Careers Services generally, about its influence with clients, and the balance between destinational options and choices in various LEAs. This view was reinforced by the observation that many Careers Services already collect good destination statistics because they themselves find it useful for their policy making, management, and information purposes. In the most sophisticated systems the information is collected for statutory school leavers, lower and upper sixth formers, YTS leavers, and FE leavers, disaggregated by such factors as sex, ethnic origin, education speciality (TVEI, CPVE) and occupational category in training or employment as appropriate. Performance could be enhanced by the further development of this aspect of the Careers Service management information system.

The report argues that the collection and dissemination of national young persons' destination statistics by a cooperative effort between Careers Service Branch and local Careers Services can provide a very useful flow of important information to debates over appropriate educational and vocational training policies. Following from this, the proposition set out in this report is simple - that each Careers Service might collect standardised annual destination statistics in the same month and that the coordination of the data collection exercise could be undertaken by the Careers Service Branch (CSB). This approach has the benefits of being simple, cost effective and relevant to policy needs at both local and national levels. At the local level it would give Principal Careers Officers and staff information on young peoples' destinations in their local authority compared to other LEAs, and trend data from year to year. LEAs could be grouped for comparison purposes. At an aggregated level it would provide CSB with a managment tool useful in discussions with DES, the Training Commission and other agencies. At a national level, the numerous requests in Parliamentary Questions for this kind of information

Conclusion

indicates its relevance to policy debates. At any level destination statistics provide information on staying-on rates into full-time education, youth employment rates, and entry rates to YTS and its relative importance compared with traditional destinations. The material would also help in any consideration of whether more YTS places need to be created, and in planning in the Non-Advanced Further Education (NAFE) sector.

One apparent advantage of this proposal is that it conforms with the general experience that where the outcome measurement is difficult or impossible, the development of increased management information flows is a useful way to proceed. A review of progress in developing output and performance indicators under the Financial Management Initiative confirmed this point. Further, while the relevance of any aspect of the information to a consideration of system performance is open to discussion, the usefulness of these statistics does not hinge on that point. On the contrary their usefulness as statistical background to current policy debates and as a pre-requisite for good management stands whatever their relevance as a performance measure. Destination statistics represent a conjunction of the Careers Service's intelligence and service functions and their absence may diminish performance.

References

Ashton, D.N. and Maguire, M. 1986, *Young Adults in the Labour Market*. London: Department of Employment, Research Paper No. 55.

Ashton, D.N.; Maguire, M. and Garland, V. 1982, *Youth in the Labour Market*. London: Department of Employment, Research Paper No. 34.

Association of Careers Advisors in Colleges of Higher Education (ACACHE) 1986, *First Destination Statistics of Students Qualifying in 1985*. Liverpool: Liverpool Institute of Higher Education.

Association of Graduate Careers Advisory Services (AGCAS) 1986, *First Destinations of Polytechnic Students Qualifying in 1985*. London: Committee of Directors of Polytechnics.

Audit Commission 1986, *Performance Review in Local Government*. London.

Ball, B. 1984, *Careers Counselling in Practice*. London: The Falmer Press.

Bedford, F.D. 1982, *Vocational Guidance Interviews Explored*. London, Department of Employment, Careers Service Branch.

Bedford, F.D. and Fort, A, 1980, *Manual for Students' Careers Interview Follow-up Form - SCIFF*. London, Department of Employment, Careers Service Branch.

Beeton, D. 1986, 'Justifying Departmental Expenditure Programmes' in *Public Money*, December, pp. 43-47.

References

Bentham, G. 1986, 'Public satisfaction and social economic and environmental conditions in the counties of England'. *Transactions Institute British Geographers.* N.S, v.11, pp.27-36.

Brennan, J. et al. 1987, 'My brilliant careers' *Times Higher Educational Supplement* 5.22.87.

Cabinet Office (MPO)/Treasury Financial Management Unit, 1985. *Policy Work and the FMI.* London: H.M. Treasury.

Carley, M. 1981, *Social Measurement and Social Indicators: Issues of Policy and Theory.* London: George Allen and Unwin.

Cherry, N. and Gear, R. 1984, *Young People's Perceptions of their Vocational Guidance Needs.* London: Department of Employment, Careers Service Branch.

Clarke, L. 1980a, *Occupational Choice: a critical review of research in the United Kingdom.* London: HMSO for Careers Service Branch, Department of Employment.

Clarke, L. 1980b, *The Transition from School to Work: a critical review of research in the United Kingdom.* London: HMSO for Careers Service Branch, Department of Employment.

Clarke, L. 1980c, *The Practice of Vocational Guidance: a critical review of research in the United Kingdom.* London: HMSO for Careers Service Branch, Department of Employment.

Clarke, M. and Stewart, J. 1985. *Local Government and the Public Service Orientation: Or Does a Public Service Provide for the Public.* Local Government Training Board.

Clarke, M. and Stewart, J. 1987, 'Movement towards a focus on service' in *Local Government Chronicle,* 2 January.

Cleaton, D. 1987, *Survey of Careers Work.* NACGT/Newpoint Publishing.

Cleveland County Council, 1986, *Citizens' Views on the Performance of their Local Authorities.*

Collin, A. and Young, R.A. 1986, 'New Directions for Theories of Career' in *Human Relations,* v.39, pp. 837-853.

Performance monitoring

Commission for Racial Equality, 1987, *Annual Report 1986*.

Department of Employment 1986, *Building Business not Barriers*. HMSO.

Employment Gazette, 1987, 'Ethnic Origin and Economic Status', January, pp. 18-29.

Flynn, N. 1986, 'Performance Measurement in Public Sector Services' in *Policy and Politics*, v.14, pp. 389-404.

Gottfredson, L.S. 1983, 'Creating and Criticizing Theory' in *Journal of Vocational Behaviour*, v.23, pp. 203-212.

Gray, A. and Jenkins, W.I. 1986, 'Accountable Management in British Central Government' in *Financial Accountability and Management*, v.2, pp. 171-186.

Gray, D. and King, S. 1986, *The Youth Training Scheme: The First Three Years*. Sheffield: MSC.

Gray, V. 1980, 'Guidance in Scottish Seconday Schools: a client evaluation' in *British Journal of Guidance and Counselling*, v.8, pp. 133-145.

Grimwood, M. and Tomkins, C. 1986, 'Value for Money Auditing - Towards Incorporating a Naturalistic Approach' in *Financial Accountability and Managment*, v.2, pp. 251-271.

Hennessy, P. 1987, 'Scrutinies bring savings, but bigger prizes await'. *Independent* (21/12).

House of Commons (Committee of Public Accounts) 1986, *Minutes of Evidence. The Financial Management Initiative*, London: HMSO (HCP 61-i).

House of Commons (Committee of Public Accounts) 1987, Session 1986- 87, *The Financial Management Initiative*, London: HMSO (HCP 61).

Hurst, K. 1985, *Patients Expectations of and Satisfaction with Nursing Care*. Central Nottingham District Health Authority.

References

Institute of Manpower Studies, 1986, 'Issues on Performance Appraisal' in *IMS News*, December.

James, A. 1987, 'Performance and the planning process' in *Social Services Insight*, March 6, pp. 12-14.

Kelly, M., Griffith, J. and Dorsman, M. 1986, *Approaches to Employment: An Investigation of Graduate Destinations*, London: CNAA.

Knapp, M., Baines, B. and Robertson, E. 1986, *The Relevance of Context Indicators for the Interpretation of Output and Performance Measures in the Careers Service*. University of Kent, Personal Social Services Research Unit, Discussion Paper 419.

LAMSAC, 1986, *Central Education Administration*. Careers Service, Research Paper No. 5, London.

Larson, R. 1978, 'Thirty Years of Research on the Subjective Well-Being of Older Americans' in *Journal of Gerontology*, v.33, pp. 109-125.

Lavercombe, S. and Fleming, D. 1981, 'Attitudes and Duration of Unemployment among Sixteen year old School Leavers' in *British Journal of Guidance and Counselling*, v.9, pp. 37-45.

Law, B. 1981, 'Community Interaction: a "Mid-Range" Focus for Theories of Career Development in Young Adults' in *British Journal of Guidance and Counselling*, v.9, pp. 142-158.

Management and Personnel Office 1986, (second edition) *Performance Measurement: A Guide for Management Services Staff*, London: Cabinet Office (MPO) MEZ.

Maguire, M.J. and Ashton, D.N. 1983, 'Changing face of the Careers Service' in *Employment Gazette*, March pp. 87-101.

Martin, E.M. 1986, 'Consumer Evaluation of Human Services' in *Social Policy and Administration*, v.20, pp. 185-200.

Metropolitan Toronto 1986, 'Corporate Performance Measurement Program'. Unpublished.

Moser, C.A. and Kalton, G. 1971, *Survey Methods in Social Investigation*, London: Heinemann.

Murgatroyd, S.J. 1977, 'Pupil Perceptions of Counselling: a Case Study' in *British Journal of Guidance and Counselling*, v.5, pp.73-78.

National Consumer Council 1986, *Measuring Up: consumer assessment of local authority services*. London.

National Audit Office (NAO) 1986, *The Financial Management Initiative*, London: HMSO, 588.

Pollitt, C. 1985, 'Measuring Performance: A New System for the National Health Service' in *Policy and Politics*, v.13, pp. 1-15.

Pollitt, C. 1986, 'Performance Measurement in the Public Services: some political implications' in *Parliamentary Affairs*, July, pp.315-329.

Porteous, M.A. and Fisher, C.J. 1980, 'Counselling, Support and Advice: the Adolescent Viewpoint' in *British Journal of Guidance and Counselling*, v.8, pp. 67- 75.

Pryor, R.G.L. 1985, 'Towards a Composite Theory of Career Development and Choice' in *British Journal of Guidance and Counselling*, v.13, pp. 225-237.

Raffe, D. 1987, 'YTS and Scottish School Leavers' in *Education and Training UK*. Policy Journals.

Ranson, S. and Ribbins, P. 1986, *The Management of Change in the Careers Service*, Birmingham: Institute of Local Government Studies.

Rhodes, R.A.W. 1987, 'Developing the Public Service Orientation' in *Local Government Studies*, v.13, pp.63-73.

Roberts, K., Dench, S. and Richardson, D. 1986, *The Changing Structure of Youth Labour Markets*, London: Department of Employment, Research Paper 59.

Ryrie, A.C. 1983, *On Leaving School*, Sevenoaks: Hodder and Stoughton.

Sawden, A., Tucker, S. and Pelican, J. 1978, *Study of the Transition from School to Working Life*, London: Youth Aid.

References

Siann, G., Draper, J. and Cosford, B. 1982, 'Pupils as Consumers: Perceptions of Guidance and Counselling in a Scottish School' in *British Journal of Guidance and Counselling*, v.10, pp. 51-61.

Social Services Inspectorate Development Group 1986. *Self Monitoring and Inspection Systems*. London: DHSS.

Steven, I.D. and Douglas, R.M. 1986, 'A Self-Contained Method of Evaluating Patient Dissatisfaction in General Practice' in *Family Practice*, v.3, pp. 14-19.

Stipak, B. 1979, 'Citizen satisfaction with urban services: potential misuse as a performance indicator', *Public Administration Review*, v.39, pp.46-52.

Stoney, S.M. and Scott, V.M. 1984, *Careers Guidance in Colleges and Polytechnics: a study of practice and provision*, Windsor: NFER-Nelson.

Super, D.E. 1980, 'A Life-Span, Life-Space Approach to Career Development' in *Journal of Vocational Behaviour*, v.16, pp.282-298.

Tarsh, J. 1987, 'What Happens to New Graduates' in *Education and Training UK*, Policy Journals.

Taylor, I. and Owen, A. 1986, *Monitoring the quality of Jobcentre Services 1985: Jobseeker Experience and Attitudes*, MSC, Psychological Service, Report No. 195/5.

H.M. Treasury, 1986. *Output and Performance Measurement in Central Government: Progress in Departments*, London: HMSO, Working Paper No. 38, S. Lewis, ed.

H.M. Treasury, 1987. *Output and Performance Measurement in Central Government: Some Practical Achievements*, London: HMSO, Working Paper No. 45, P. Durham, ed.

University Grants Committee (UGC) 1986, *First Destinations of University Graduates*, Cheltenham: Universities' Statistical Record.

vondracek, F.W, Lerner, R.M. and Schulenberg, J.E. 1983a, 'The Concept of Development in Vocational Theory and Intervention' in *Journal of Vocational Behaviour*, v.23, pp. 179-202.

Vondracek, F.W., Lerner, R.M. and Schulenberg, J.E. 1983b, 'On Aspiring to Present a Developmental Theory of Occupational Aspirations' in *Journal of Vocational Behaviour*, v.23, pp.213-218.

Walker, P. and Dunn, R. 1987, 'Performance indicators: how does your district shape up?' *The Health Service Journal*, 9 July.

Wallace, A. and Rees, S. 1984, 'The Priority of Client Evaluations' in *Research Highlights No. 8 Evaluation*, Aberdeen: Department of Social Work.

Ware, M.E. 1980, 'Antecedents of Educational/Career Preferences and Choices' in *Journal of Vocational Behaviour*, v.16, pp. 312-319.

Watts, A.G., Super, D.E. and Kidd, J.M. 1981, *Career Development in Britain*, Cambridge: Hobsons Press.

Webber, R.J. 1979, *Census Enumeration Districts: A Socio-Economic Classification*, London: OPCS.

West, M. and Newton, P. 1983. *The Transition from School to Work*. London: Croom Helm.

Waynes, D.K. 1987, 'On Assessing Efficiency in the Provision of Local Authority Services' in *Local Government Studies*, Jan/Feb, pp. 53-68.

Appendices

A. The objectives and methods of the study
B. Functions of local authority Careers Services
C. Sample destination statistics in local authorities
D. The Careers Service Management Return (CSMR) and sample output
E. Sample statutory leavers destination questionnaire
F. Sample graduate leaver questionnaire
G. Sample tables generated by FDS
H. Sample material on destination statistics from selected local authorities

Appendix A:
The objectives and methods of the study

Introduction

This study was intended to review the options available to the Careers Service Branch of the Department of Employment for assessing performance in the delivery of careers services in England and Wales and to assist the Branch in meeting its objectives under the Financial Management Initiative. The focus of the project is both on the potential for inter-authority comparisons of performance, and on the means for intra-authority enhancement of performance.

At the outset of the research project, the Careers Service Branch (CSB) requested that the Policy Studies Institute (PSI) study the feasibility of developing statistical instruments to measure the expectations of clients of the Careers Service, and how far these were being met. Clients were defined as:

a) employers;

b) YTS managing agents;

c) careers teachers, heads and college principals; and

d) young people in school, in training and in employment.

Parents of young people could also be seen as clients of the careers service but were excluded from consideration as their needs were to be considered in a later study.

The terms of reference specified that the thrust of the project was towards developing a management and policy instrument which could provide the Careers Service with reliable information about its performance. A basic assumption of the research effort therefore was that the satisfaction measures devised were to be useful in a regular, periodic inter-local authority performance (LEA) monitoring system. If successful this study of expectations and satisfactions was to form the first part of an exercise to design a range of methodologically sound tools for measuring performance. In pursuing this the Careers Service Branch hoped to be able to comply in full with the objectives of the Financial Management Initiative (FMI) in central government.

At the midpoint of the project, an interim report suggested a number of reasons why the measurement of expectations and satisfactions of clients as part of a regular inter-authority monitoring system would face severe methodological and political difficulties. In particular these stemmed from the difficulty of measuring the outcome of vocational guidance services, and from the near impossibility of standardising the situation of LEAs so as to allow some subsequent assessment of relative performance in service delivery. In particular there are dramatic differences among the 96 local education authorities in England in terms of political and professional priorities, resource base and allocation, and differing labour market and socio-demographic contexts.

In the interim report it was suggested that measurement of client satisfactions, although important to any assessment of performance, was best done as part of a specific examination of Careers Service activities within local education authorities rather than as a tool for inter-authority comparisons, or used as an aggregate measure of overall performance. In light of this the interim report suggested that further attempts to devise reliable and valid measures of comparative satisfaction might not be the best use of resources. However, during this first phase of the research on client satisfaction, considerable work also had been done on reviewing the possibilities for performance monitoring in general. The Careers Service Branch noted that recurring attempts to devise performance measures of the Careers Service had foundered for one reason or another and therefore accepted the researcher's suggestion that a general review of the options for performance monitoring might be an appropriate focus for the remainder of the research project. The report has documented all aspects of the research process.

Methodology of the study

The general methodological approach has been literature review, key informant interviews, and group discussions with staff of the careers service and with representatives of its various clients groups. Two rounds of fieldwork have taken place. The first, in the autumn of 1986 focussed on the expectations and satisfactions of clients of the careers service. The second round, in mid 1987, addressed more general questions of performance monitoring.

In detail the research activities have consisted first, of a broad review of the academic literature on vocational guidance and performance monitoring since 1975. Second, preliminary key informant interviews were conducted with officers of the Careers Service Branch, its Inspectorate, and other Department of Employment (DE) representatives. Subsequent advice was given at regular meetings between a departmental steering group and the researcher. Third, during the second phase of the research, additional interviews which focussed on performance monitoring and the implementation of the Financial Management Initiative in central government were carried out at H.M. Treasury and elsewhere.

Fourth, and perhaps most important, the researcher undertook a first round of extensive fieldwork within twelve LEA Careers Services, mainly in the autumn of 1986. The underlying theme of the research activities at that point was to assess the feasibility of measuring clients' expectations and satisfactions, and the likely validity and reliability that could be expected from any measurement or interpretation of these expectations/satisfaction. It was also felt important to address any organisational or political difficulties that might be encountered in attempting to make use of such information for the purposes of inter-authority performance monitoring.

The first round of fieldwork itself consisted of observations of the operations and activities of Careers Services and numerous helpful discussions with all Principal Careers Officers and, in some cases, Assistant Principal Careers Officers (PCOs, APCOs), generic and specialist Careers Officers, Employment Assistants and receptionists in the following local authorities:

Birmingham
Bradford
London Borough of Bromley*
Devon
East Sussex
London Borough of Haringey
London Borough of Havering
Humberside*
Inner London Education Authority
Oldham*
Somerset
Surrey*

In particular those local authorities marked with an '*' were asked to allow the researcher to spend a number of days in participant observation in their schools, careers centres and elsewhere, and to interview their Careers Service staff and their clients. During these sessions the researcher sat in on 28 vocational guidance interviews in 5th form and in further and higher education (FHE), attended 7 student group guidance sessions, 1 YTS/FHE opportunities conference, and 1 YTS managing agents' forum. In addition, group discussions were arranged with senior staff, line career officers and employment assistants. In total, key informant interviews were carried out with 44 local authority careers service staff and group discussions held with a further 30 staff.

The second round (1987) of Careers Service staff interviews provided an opportunity for the researcher to report back to the PCOs and APCOs contacted in the first round. This was to discuss the findings of the study and to get their views, and those of other senior and/or statistical staff, on the proposals for additions to the Careers Service management information system, which are made in Chapter 7. The research approach of two interviews separated by about six months (and punctuated by the sending out of an interim report, a subsequent memo from the researcher, and a number of telephone conversations) constituted a kind of dialogue between the researcher and about thirty senior careers service staff in local authorities, in addition to the continuing dialogue between the researcher and the members of his CSB/DE steering group.

These activities were complemented by the interviews and group work with clients of the Careers Service. All of these were conducted in the four local authorities specified above and in some cases appointments were arranged with the assistance of the Principal or Assistant Principal Careers Officers. YTS managing agents were interviewed at their offices. Careers teachers and heads were interviewed while the researcher was in each of eight schools observing vocational guidance interviews and group sessions. Where a school head was not interviewed, usually due to their time constraint, a short introduction was arranged by a careers teacher. Young people in education were interviewed in schools, singly and in groups. Those in YTS were interviewed at careers offices. Finally, the first two employers were interviewed in person. However it was found that there was insufficient material to be covered to warrant further face-to-face interviews and the remainder of interviews with employers were conducted over the telephone. A total of 75 interviews were conducted with clients of the Careers Service. Further details of the numbers of interviews carried out and the types of persons interviewed are listed below:

Interviews with Careers Services' clients

10 employers
12 YTS managing agents
9   careers teachers
4   school heads
24 young people in education

9   young people on YTS
7   young people in the labour market

Interviews with Careers Service staff
12 Principal Careers Officers
11 Assistant Principal Careers Officers
12 Careers Officers
5   Employment Assistants
4   Receptionists

Group Sessions
7   Group guidance in schools
1   Managing agents
2   With Careers Officers and Employment Assistants

Monitoring of trainees: blanket or sampling or none?
Racial monitoring of YTS

Employers
Labour market surveys, geographic or sectoral
Placement
Industrial visits
Coordination with economic development units
Coordination of work experience programmes

The unemployed
Unemployed outreach work
Job clubs
Coordination of community unemployment activities
Counselling at Job Centres

Adults
Adult guidance
Occupational or psychometric testing

Other
Racial monitoring
Publications

Appendix B: Functions of local authority Careers Services

Careers Service activities with:

Young people
Option choice work (3rd year)
Introductory lectures (fourth and early fifth year)
Group vocational work
Group guidance interviews
Individual interviews
Written follow-up

Career teachers
Curriculum development
Careers library service
Parent evenings and opportunity days
Coordination of work experience programmes

YTS managing agents/Training Commission
Provision of information on programmes
Organisation of YTS conventions
Coordination of YTS application procedures
YTS market intelligence
Development of training modules

Appendix C:
Sample destination statistics in local authorities

First destinations of school leavers in study areas: 1986 (in descending order of YTS take-up)

Percentages	HU	OLD	DE	BI	BR	ES	HAV	SUR	IN
Stayed in education	36	28	42	41	35	47	42	53	45
Entered employment	16	13	14	12	20	21	36	25	21
Entered YTS	41	37	35	33	26	18	16	9	8
Unemployed	6	12	4	14	10	4	5	3	10
Moved/other	-	3	5	-	4	2	-	-	3
Unknown	-	7	14	-	5	9	-	-	12

Note: These statistics are not comparable and are not to be quoted.

Appendix D:
The Careers Service Management Return (CSMR) and sample output

Careers Service Management Return (CSMR)
Note: Guidance on completing the CSMR is in Section G of the Careers Service Manual

Name of Local Education Authority .... Name of Careers Office .... Statistical Code Number

Return for period of four / five weeks from .... to ....

Prepared by .... (Name and telephone number) Approved by .... (officer in charge)

Copies sent to Careers Service Branch on .... (date) and to the Principal Careers Officer

Table 1 Careers Service and Young People in Full-time Education

Table 1(a) Work with pupils and students in full-time education

| England and Wales | Maintained schools ||| Independent Schools | Colleges || Total (1)-(6) |
| Scotland | Pre 5th year | 5th year | Post 5th year | | NAFE | AFE + HE | |
	Pre S4 (1)	S4 (2)	Post S4 (3)	(4)	(5)	(6)	(7)
1 Interview by Careers Officers							
2 Interviews by other staff							
3 Small group sessions							
4 Class size and other group sessions							

Table 1(b) Work with parents

	School pupils (1)	College students (2)	Total (1) and (2) (3)		School pupils (5)	College students (6)	Total (5) and (6) (7)
5 Interviews				parent(s) present (included in lines (1) and (2)) / parent(s) only			
6 Small group sessions				parent(s) present (included in line (3)) / parent(s) only			
7 Class size and other group sessions				parent(s) present (included in line (4)) / parent(s) only			

CSMR

Table 2 - Careers Service and the Labour Market

2(a) Work with full-time education leavers, the unemployed, YTS trainees and the employed

	Full-time education leavers		Unemployed (with some employment after FTE)			YTS Trainees	Employed			Total (1) to (9)
	Under 18 (1)	18 and over (2)	Under 18 (3)	18-24 (4)	25 and over (5)	(6)	Under 18 (7)	18-24 (8)	25 and over (9)	(10)
8 Interviews by Careers officers										
9 Interviews by other staff										
10 Small group sessions										
11 Other group sessions										
12 Placings into jobs										
13 Placings onto YTS										

2(b) Client stocks and flow

	Full-time education leavers		Unemployed (with some employment after FTE)			YTS Trainees	Employed			Total (1) to (9)
	Under 18 (1)	18 and over (2)	Under 18 (3)	18-24 (4)	25 and over (5)	(6)	Under 18 (7)	18-24 (8)	25 and over (9)	(10)
14 Total at end of previous period										
15 Flow in during period										
16 Total at end of this period										

2(c) Work with employers and training providers

	Unfilled at end of previous period (1)	Notified in period (2)	Filled in period by Careers Service (3)	Unfilled at end of this period (4)
17 Job vacancies				

18 Employers and training providers visited	

CSMR (9/87)

Department of Employment
Careers Service Branch
HQR.9.87

DATE 15/04/87 PROGRAM GH04
CAREERS SERVICE
AGGREGATED RETURNS FOR ENGLAND FOR PERIOD 13/02/87 - 12/03/87

TABLE 1A

	ENGLAND & WALES SCOTLAND	MAINTAINED SCHOOLS PRE 5TH YEAR PRE S4 (1)	MAINTAINED SCHOOLS 5TH YEAR S4 (2)	MAINTAINED SCHOOLS POST 5TH YEAR POST S4 (3)	INDEPENDENT SCHOOLS (4)	COLLEGES NAFE (5)	COLLEGES AFE + HE (6)	TOTAL (1)-(6) (7)
1 INTERVIEW BY CAREERS OFFICERS		4044	91229	15044	2046	7358	1320	121041
2 INTERVIEWS BY OTHER STAFF		630	12941	1100	42	1823	829	17365
3 SMALL GROUP SESSIONS		520	3470	559	45	296	65	4955
4 CLASS SIZE AND OTHER GROUP SESSIONS		912	1842	426	41	219	63	3503

TABLE 1B

	PARENTS PRESENT SCHOOL PUPILS (1)	PARENTS PRESENT COLLEGE STUDENTS (2)	PARENTS PRESENT TOTAL (1) & (2) (3)	PARENTS ONLY SCHOOL PUPILS (5)	PARENTS ONLY COLLEGE STUDENTS (6)	PARENTS ONLY TOTAL (5) & (6) (7)
5 INTERVIEWS	13859	549	14408	8609	476	9085
6 SMALL GROUP SESSIONS	202	11	213	182	5	187
7 CLASS SIZE AND OTHER GROUP SESSIONS	347	12	359	284	32	316

TABLE 2A

	FULL-TIME EDUCATION LEAVERS UNDER 18 (1)	FULL-TIME EDUCATION LEAVERS 18 AND OVER (2)	UNEMPLOYED (WITH SOME EMPLOYMENT AFTER FTE) UNDER 18 (3)	UNEMPLOYED 18-24 (4)	UNEMPLOYED 25 & OVER (5)	YTS TRAINEES (6)	EMPLOYED UNDER 18 (7)	EMPLOYED 18-24 (8)	EMPLOYED 25 AND OVER (9)	TOTAL (1) TO (9) (10)
8 INTERVIEWS BY CAREERS OFFICERS	11925	2787	9068	4377	1896	12311	1205	2076	1428	47073
9 INTERVIEWS BY OTHER STAFF	27090	4170	20981	5313	548	8347	2496	1331	334	70610
10 SMALL GROUP SESSIONS	171	30	324	297	62	604	19	8	12	1527
11 OTHER GROUP SESSIONS	75	1	17	34	21	154	2	1	4	309
12 PLACINGS INTO JOBS	1633	373	1730	418	15	690	255	241	2	5357
13 PLACINGS ONTO YTS	2942	109	689	39	1	493	55	5	0	4333

TABLE 2B

	UNFILLED AT END OF PREV PERIOD	NOTIFIED IN PERIOD	FILLED IN PERIOD	UNFILLED AT END OF THIS PERIOD
14 TOTAL AT END OF PREVIOUS PERIOD	65074	19113	29826	10250
15 FLOW IN DURING PERIOD	6495	1457	5955	97
16 TOTAL AT END OF THIS PERIOD	59335	18084	28795	10674

TABLE 2C

	UNFILLED AT END OF PREV PERIOD	NOTIFIED IN PERIOD	FILLED IN PERIOD	UNFILLED AT END OF THIS PERIOD
17 JOB VACANCIES	11760	9469	5068	12204
18 YTS PLACES	28634	4430	3355	27601
19 EMPLOYERS AND TRAINING PROVIDERS	13886			

Appendix E:
Sample statutory leavers destination questionnaire

Careers Service

This form is designed to give you the opportunity to record basic details about yourself, your education, interests and any career ideas.

PLEASE COMPLETE IN BLOCK CAPITALS.

SURNAME	
FIRST NAMES	
ADDRESS	

SEX [ ] Please enter M or F

FOR CAREERS SERVICE USE ONLY

POST CODE	TELEPHONE NUMBER	DATE OF BIRTH
SCHOOL / COLLEGE		FORM
PROBABLE DATE OF LEAVING SCHOOL / COLLEGE		

DISTRICT CODE	
SCHOOL CODE	
YEAR CODE	
LEAVING YEAR	

COURSE DETAILS Please list below the subjects you are studying or have studied and tick the appropriate level.

SUBJECT	G.C.S.E.	C.S.E	'O' Level	'A' Level	Other (C.P.V.E./ B.T.E.C. etc	Mock Exam Result	Date of Final Exam	Final Grade	Exam. Code	Grade Code	Subject Code

FOR CAREERS SERVICE USE ONLY

CAREER CHOICE CODES

Level of Attainment	
No. of Subjects	
Present Situation	
JC/SL	
Y.T.S. Status	
NOTE	

Please turn ove[r]

Bromley
THE LONDON BOROUGH

PS 2808

Please list here (a) the subjects you like most

(b) your strongest subjects

(c) subjects which you find particularly difficult

INTERESTS Please list those activities in which you participate, giving details of any special responsibilities or prizes/awards.

EMPLOYMENT Please list any full or part-time employment or work experience you have had.

CAREER CHOICE Which careers are you considering?

FURTHER EDUCATION Are you considering any full-time courses at school or college? If yes, please give details.

If there are any special factors which affect your future plans (e.g. leaving the area, health, etc.) please note them here.

If there are any questions or requests for information which you or your parents wish to discuss with the Careers Officer, please note them here.

Your Signature .... Date ....

Name of Parent or Guardian ....

Appendix F:
Sample graduate leaver questionnaire

University of London Careers Advisory Service

First Destination Return 1985-86

I understand that you will be finishing your degree studies this year and I am writing to ask for your co-operation in completing the Careers Advisory Service's important annual First Destination Return.

The purpose of this survey is to collect information about what happens to students after they graduate; for example, how many go straight into employment, take a year off, go on to further training, etc. The identification of trends (and fields in which particular problems are encountered) is an essential step towards helping us to give better careers advice to those who come after you into higher education, as well as enabling us to influence government attitudes to graduate employment and training.

This survey is not intended to be an intrusion of your privacy, and great care is taken to ensure that no information about you personally can be obtained from any published statistics. I should be most grateful if you would help us by completing the following questionnaire and returning it as quickly as possible. Any information you can give, no matter how indefinite your plans may be at present, will be most helpful.

Finally, may I take this opportunity to wish you every success in your future, and to remind you that the Careers Advisory Service will be glad to give you any assistance it can, now and at any time in the future. (Please see the reverse of this form for details).

B. E. Steptoe
Director

Section I

PLEASE ANSWER ALL QUESTIONS IN THIS SECTION (BUT 9 AND 10 FOR HIGHER DEGREE GRADUATES ONLY)

1 Title, eg Rev, Dr, Mrs, Ms ....

2 Surname...

3 Previous surname ....

4 Other name ....

5 Address ....

   ....

6 College, Institute or School ....

7 Subject(s) ....

8 Qualification, eg BA, BSc (Eng), MSc, PhD ....

9 Date higher degree awarded (if applicable) ....

10 Higher degree graduates — please state how your course was financed, eg Research Council grant, bank loan, personal savings, charity, etc.

   ....

   ....

   ....

Section II

PLEASE COMPLETE *ALL* DETAILS IN WHICHEVER QUESTION(S) APPLY TO YOU

1 **If you have entered/will be entering employment:—**

   Date employment started/starts ....

   Name and Activities of Employer...

   ....

   Job Title and Type of Work ....

   ....

   Location of Post ....

   ....

   Salary (if you are prepared to state it) ....

   Will the job last more than three months? ....

   How and where did you find out about this vacancy, eg Job Opportunities Bulletin, 'Milkround', etc.

   ....

   ....

2 **If you have entered/will be entering a course of study or training:—**

   Date study/training started/starts ....

   Name of institution ....

   Qualification sought, eg PGCE, MSc ....

   Principal subject or nature of training ....

   ....

   Please specify how this course will be financed, eg Research Council grant, bank loan, personal savings, charity, etc.

   ....

3 If you have *not* entered employment or study/training:—

  Are you unemployed? ....

  Are you unavailable for, or not seeking, employment or study/training? (Please state why)

  ....

  Are you an Overseas graduate leaving the UK? If yes, please state to which country you are going

  ....

4 If your circumstances are not covered by any of the above alternatives, please give details below

  ....
  ....
  ....

Section III

If you would be prepared to help the Careers Advisory Service with further surveys connected with this project, or with follow-up surveys in the future, please complete the address label below. Please give an address through which you think it likely we will be able to contact you in twelve months' time.

  Name ....

  Address ....
  ....
  ....
  ....

THANK YOU FOR YOUR CO-OPERATION

CAREERS SERVICE FACILITIES YOU MAY WISH TO USE

The University of London Careers Advisory Service offers a free careers guidance and employment service to students, graduates and postgraduates of the University. In addition to the comprehensive information and reference library facilities at Central Office in Gordon Square, the service includes the issue of a weekly 'Job Opportunities Bulletin', the distribution of 'Current Vacancies' which is produced fortnightly by the Central Services Unit, and the operation of an Availability Register of graduates of the last three years who are currently available for employment or who are seeking a change of employment.

If you are undecided about your career or have been unable to obtain the type of employment you are seeking, then you may want to have a discussion with a careers adviser, but please note that the University of London cannot assist in any way with the cost of travel or any associated expenses you may incur in coming to Gordon Square or your College Careers Office. Alternatively, if you live outside the London area, you may prefer to use the advisory services provided by a university or polytechnic careers service nearer your home. Unfortunately we do not have information on careers services outside the UK.

If you would like information on any of the above facilities please telephone 01-387 8221 and ask for the Registration Section, except in the case of the Availability Register when you should ask for the Employer Relations Section. If you live a long way from London you may prefer to write to us at the address below.

SECOND FOLD HERE

Postage will be paid by licensee

Do not affix Postage Stamps if posted in Gt Britain, Channel Islands, N Ireland or the Isle of Man

BUSINESS REPLY SERVICE
Licence No WC 502

B. E. Steptoe, Esq.
Director,
University of London Careers Advisory Service
50 Gordon Square
LONDON
WC1H 0BR

THIRD FOLD HERE AND TUCK IN

Appendix G:
Sample tables generated by FDS

TABLE 2 CLASSIFICATION OF STUDENT DESTINATIONS BY COURSES
(Degree and Diploma excluding Initial Teacher Training Courses)

COURSES		Employment - Home Permanent	Home Short Term	Overseas Permanent	Overseas Short Term	Already in employment	Total	Research Home	Research Overseas	First degree courses — home	Law Society and Bar Exams	Other training	Teacher training	Total	Overseas students leaving UK	Not available for employment	Believed unemployed as at 31.12.84	Total known respondents	Unknown	Total in Survey
Higher Degrees		10	0	0	0	5	15	0	0	0	0	0	0	0	2	0	0	17	1	18
	%	58.8	0.0	0.0	0.0	29.4	88.2	0.0	0.0	0.0	0.0	0.0	0.0	0.0	11.8	0.0	0.0	100		
Post-Graduate Diplomas		89	7	3	0	0	99	0	0	0	0	1	0	1	3	3	1	107	41	148
	%	83.2	6.5	2.8	0.0	0.0	92.5	0.0	0.0	0.0	0.0	0.9	0.0	0.9	2.8	2.8	0.9	100		
Bachelor Degrees B.A.		1555	209	78	16	1	1859	157	9	3	101	328	371	969	53	106	551	3538	679	4217
	%	44.0	5.9	2.2	0.5	0.0	52.5	4.4	0.2	0.1	28.6	9.3	10.5	27.4	1.4	3.0	15.6	100		
B Sc		222	28	7	3	10	270	24	0	0	0	12	34	70	31	13	53	437	118	555
	%	50.8	6.4	1.6	0.6	2.3	61.8	0.4	0.0	0.0	0.0	2.7	7.8	16.0	7.1	3.0	12.1	100		
Other		402	75	16	9	1	503	21	1	0	9	85	124	240	7	17	155	922	137	1059
	%	43.6	8.1	1.7	1.0	0.1	54.6	2.3	0.1	0.0	1.0	9.2	2.6	26.0	0.7	1.8	16.8	100		
Total Bachelor Degrees		2179	312	101	28	12	2632	202	10	3	110	425	529	1279	91	136	759	4897	934	5831
	%	44.5	6.4	2.1	0.5	0.2	53.7	4.1	0.2	0.1	2.2	8.7	10.8	26.1	1.9	2.7	15.4	100		
Higher Diplomas		1127	61	32	11	42	1273	5	2	80	2	144	5	238	155	10	181	1857	621	2478
	%	60.7	3.3	1.7	0.6	2.3	68.6	0.2	0.1	4.3	0.1	7.8	0.2	12.8	8.3	0.5	9.7	100		
Dip. H.E.		9	0	0	0	0	9	0	0	382	0	2	110	494	0	4	9	516	49	565
	%	1.7	0.0	0.0	0.0	0.0	1.7	0.0	0.0	74.0	0.0	0.3	21.3	95.7	0.0	0.7	1.7	100		
Other Diplomas		435	14	11	4	35	499	7	4	8	0	13	5	37	28	10	45	619	215	834
	%	70.2	2.3	1.8	0.6	5.7	80.6	1.1	0.6	1.2	0.0	2.1	0.8	6.0	4.5	1.6	7.3	100		
Totals		3849	394	147	43	94	4527	214	16	473	112	585	649	2049	279	163	995	8013	1861	9874
	%	48.0	4.9	1.8	0.5	1.2	56.5	2.7	0.2	5.9	1.4	7.3	8.1	25.6	3.5	2.0	12.4	100		

Percentages are of total known.

TABLE 3 CLASSIFICATION OF STUDENTS BY EMPLOYER CATEGORIES
(Degrees and Diplomas, excluding Initial Teacher Training)

Home Employment (Permanent) and Already in Employment

COURSES	Public Service: Civil Service	HM Forces	Local/Public Authorities	Total	% Total entering home employment	Education: Schools	FE Estabs.	Polytechnics	Universities	Total	% Total entering home employment	Industry and Commerce: Agriculture Forestry, Fisheries	Oil, Mining Chemical Ind.	Engineering and allied	Other Manufacturing	Building, Civil Eng. Architect	Public utilities	Accountancy	Banking Insurance Finance	Other Commerce	Total	% Total entering permanent home employment	Miscellaneous: Private Practice	Leisure Entertainment	Others	Total	% Total entering permanent home employment	Unknown	Total entering perm. home employment
Higher Degrees	2	0	0	2	13.3	7	0	0	0	7	46.7	0	0	0	2	0	0	0	0	1	3	20.0	1	0	1	2	13.3	1	15
Post-Graduate Diplomas	3	0	13	16	18.0	0	1	2	6	9	10.1	2	4	7	6	2	0	0	3	15	39	43.8	2	7	10	19	21.3	6	89
Bachelor Degrees B.A.	106	14	212	332	21.3	48	37	41	11	137	8.8	7	18	47	88	25	55	39	52	372	703	45.2	17	117	189	323	20.8	61	1556
B.Sc.	14	6	74	94	40.5	4	0	11	1	16	6.9	1	6	12	13	8	11	4	6	34	95	40.1	0	0	14	14	6.0	13	232
Other	3	3	18	24	22.4	9	1	4	0	15	14.0	0	1	1	2	0	2	2	5	26	39	36.4	8	8	6	22	20.6	7	107
B.A./B.Sc.	15	4	44	63	21.3	12	5	4	0	21	7.1	0	1	7	10	1	11	3	16	79	128	43.2	5	25	46	76	25.7	8	296
Higher Diplomas	37	4	104	145	12.4	20	9	15	3	47	4.0	6	39	193	81	31	127	17	62	292	848	72.5	2	30	48	80	6.8	49	1169
Dip. H.E.	1	0	2	3	33.3	0	0	0	0	0	0.0	0	0	0	0	0	1	0	0	2	3	33.3	1	1	0	2	22.2	1	9
Other Diplomas	5	2	256	263	56.0	3	1	0	0	4	0.9	0	1	10	19	14	23	13	13	39	132	28.0	25	16	30	71	15.1	0	470
Totals	186	33	723	942	23.9	103	54	77	22	256	6.5	16	70	277	221	81	230	78	157	860	1990	50.5	61	204	344	609	15.4	146	3943

TABLE 4 CLASSIFICATION OF "TYPE OF WORK" BY COURSE
(Degrees and Diplomas excluding Initial Teacher Training Courses)

Home Employment (Permanent) and Already in Employment

COURSES	Admin, Operational Management	Scientific Research Design Development	Engineering Research Design Development	Scientific Engineering Support Service	Environmental Planning	Buying Marketing Selling	Management Services	Financial Work	Legal Work	Information and Library work	Personnel	Social, Medical Security Services	Teaching and Lecturing	Creative and Entertainment	Artistic Design	Others	Unknown	Total entering perm home employment
Higher Degrees	0	0	0	0	0	0	0	0	0	0	0	0	7	0	7	0	1	15
Post Graduate Diplomas	3	0	0	0	0	14	2	0	0	19	2	0	1	1	0	47	0	89
Bachelor Degrees B.A.	251	5	6	15	24	224	23	125	7	55	19	173	71	103	197	214	44	1556
B.Sc.	39	13	8	30	10	17	3	14	0	5	5	53	7	2	1	17	8	232
Other	67	1	0	5	3	77	3	25	6	7	4	77	20	33	12	60	3	403
Total Bachelor Degrees	357	19	14	50	37	318	29	164	13	67	28	303	98	138	210	291	55	2191
Higher Diplomas	260	15	74	58	51	177	139	85	2	14	13	12	24	15	76	127	27	1169
Dip. HE	0	0	0	1	0	0	0	0	0	0	0	1	0	1	0	5	1	9
Other Diplomas	23	0	3	0	14	12	21	37	3	0	24	252	7	8	31	29	6	470
Totals	643	34	91	109	102	521	191	286	18	100	67	568	137	163	324	499	90	3943

Table 10: Unemployment and Degree Subjects, 1985

Degree subject	Unemployment rate	Degree subject	Unemployment rate
university men	%	History	29
All-subject average	15	Philosophy	46
		Theology	17
Chemical eng.	12	Arts general	28
Civil eng.	8	*polytechnic men and women*	
Electrical eng.	6	All-subject average	22
Mechanical eng.	7		
Biology	34	Biological sci.	31
Botany	42	Chemistry	25
Zoology	47	Other sci.	39
Biochemistry	27	Biol. & phys. sci.	32
Other bio. sci.	29	Maths	19
Maths/computing	10	Computing	6
Physics	17	Management sci.	5
Chemistry	20	Business & commerce	14
Geology	26	Economics	27
Bio. phys. sci.	26	Accountancy	7
Business studies	8	Geography	37
Economics	16	Law	33
Accountancy	4	Psychology	35
Geography	25	Sociology	39
Gov't & pub. admin	31	Other social stud.	37
Law	18	English	53
Psychology	35	Other languages	33
Sociology	33	History	46
Soc. sci. cmbs	21	Arts general	43
Soc. sci. with arts	26	Art and design	39
English	36	Design	22
French	24	Civil eng.	17
Classics	33	Electrical eng.	10
Languages & arts	31	Mechanical eng.	14

(Source: Tarsh, 1987)

Appendix H:
Sample material on destination statistics from selected local authorities

CITY OF BIRMINGHAM CAREERS SERVICE

SECTION 1 – DESTINATIONS OF YOUNG PEOPLE REACHING STATUTORY SCHOOL-LEAVING AGE.

This section is based upon a follow-up of all 16 year old fifth year leavers from Birmingham in 1986.

THE SAMPLE

The total group is shown below broken down by gender and ethnic origin.

	Asian Origin	Afro-Caribbean Origin	Other Non-white Origin	White Ethnic Origin	TOTALS
Male	1,560	520	85	6,192	8,357
Female	1,318	515	83	5,981	7,897
TOTALS	2,878	1,035	168	12,173	16,254

Total Sample is 16,254 of whom 14,655 had known destinations; the remaining 1,599 include those who have left the area, are not seeking or did not respond to intensive follow-up.

The main observation on these overall destination figures is that the total numbers (and percentage of the cohort) going into Y.T.S. has dropped for the second year in a row. The percentage of the fifth year group continuing in full-time education has remained at a consistent 36% over the last three years.

THE OVERALL DESTINATIONS

POST-16 DESTINATION OF THE COHORT 1986
WHICH REACHED SCHOOL LEAVING AGE

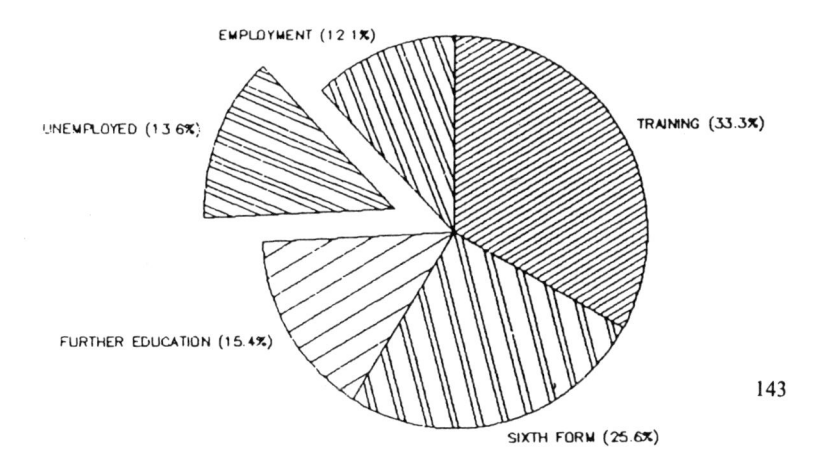

EMPLOYMENT (12.1%)
UNEMPLOYED (13.6%)
TRAINING (33.3%)
FURTHER EDUCATION (15.4%)
SIXTH FORM (25.6%)

POST-16 DESTINATION OF THE COHORT 1986
WHICH REACHED SCHOOL LEAVING AGE

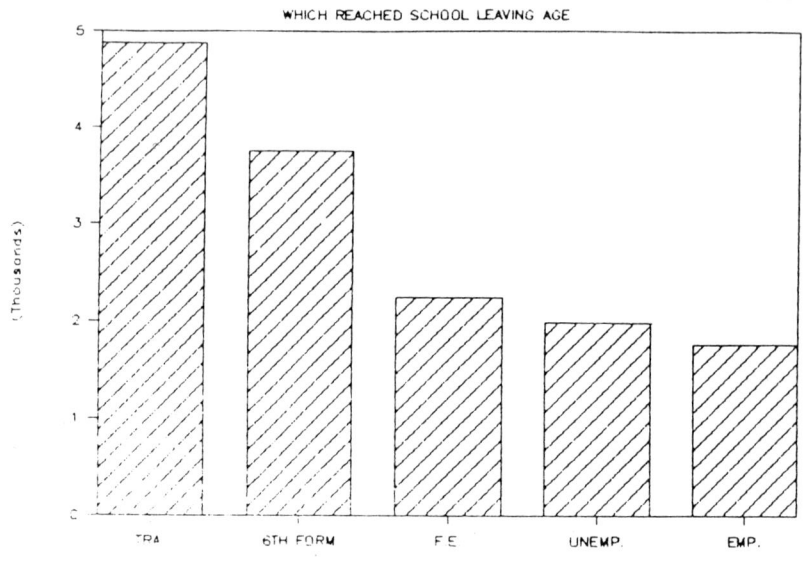

ENTRY INTO EMPLOYMENT

1,771 16 year olds went directly into employment confirming that employers generally prefer to recruit people with skills and/or experience who could quickly become productive workers.

The table below shows the range of occupations entered by school leavers and the numbers of technician and craft level jobs within these overall totals.

Occupational Classification	Full-time Employment	Of whom Craft	Tech
Engineering (including motor vehicle)	558	110	60
Woodworking occupations	26	6	0
Working in other materials (incl. textiles, plastics)	104	11	3
Construction operations	146	80	4
Farming, Gardening, Working with animals or related occupations	20	1	2
Transport/Warehouse	113	15	1
Armed Forces & Custodial Services	28	18	4
Scientific occupations	6	2	2
Medical, Nursing and allied	11	6	2
Personal Services (Hairdressing/Catering etc.)	134	18	0
Sales occupations	234	17	2
Arts/Media & related occupations	14	4	0
Admin./Clerical/Office based occupations	367	98	53
TOTALS	1771	388	133

SECTION 2 - Y.T.S. DESTINATIONS

The purpose of this section of the report is to outline what happened to young people from Birmingham leaving one year Y.T.S. from the 1985-6 programme up to October 1986.

1986 marked the transition from one year to two year Y.T.S. and so a second year of Y.T.S., through continuation places, was available to those unable to find employment at the end of their first year of training.

The existence of these continuation places had a significant effect on the destination patterns of 1986 Y.T.S. leavers.

The section is based upon an extensive survey of 8,188 Y.T.S. trainees who were followed up during and after their period on Y.T.S. to determine what happened to them when they left Y.T.S.

Almost 80 of the sample responded to the survey (those who did not include many non-Birmingham young people returning to their home areas) and the details given are based upon these responses.

WHERE DID THEY GO? - THE MAIN DESTINATIONS OF Y.T.S. LEAVERS

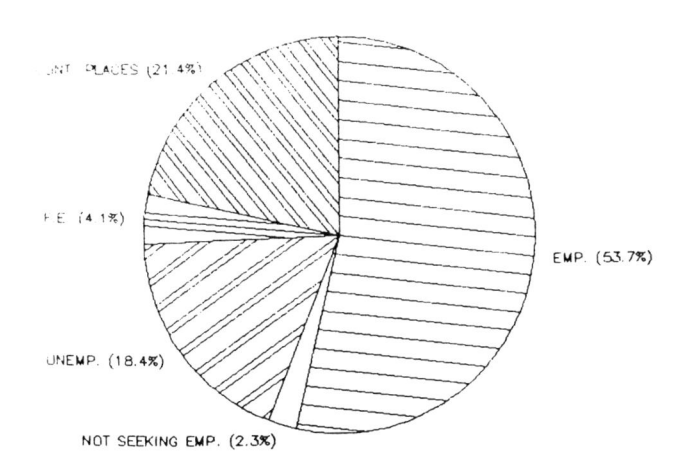

CONT. PLACES (21.4%)
F.E. (4.1%)
EMP. (53.7%)
UNEMP. (18.4%)
NOT SEEKING EMP. (2.3%)

% OF YTS LEAVERS ENTERING FURTHER Y.T.S. TRAINING

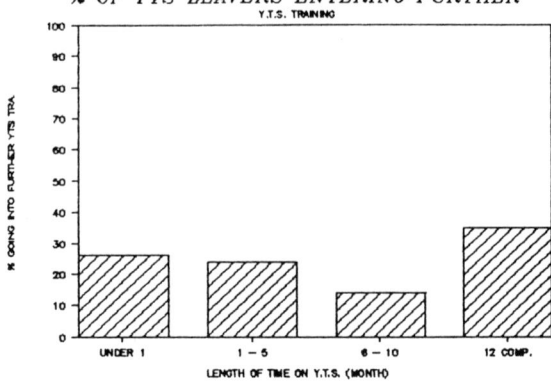

% OF YTS LEAVERS ENTERING F.E.

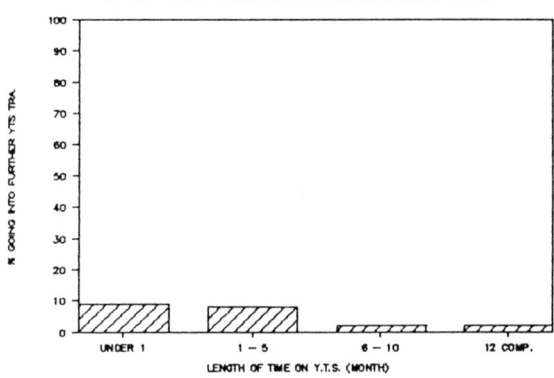

% OF YTS LEAVERS BECOMING UNEMPLOYED

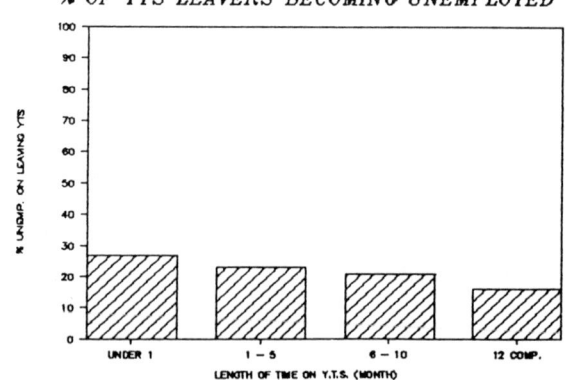

DESTINATIONS OF Y.T.S. LEAVERS BY OCCUPATIONAL GROUPS

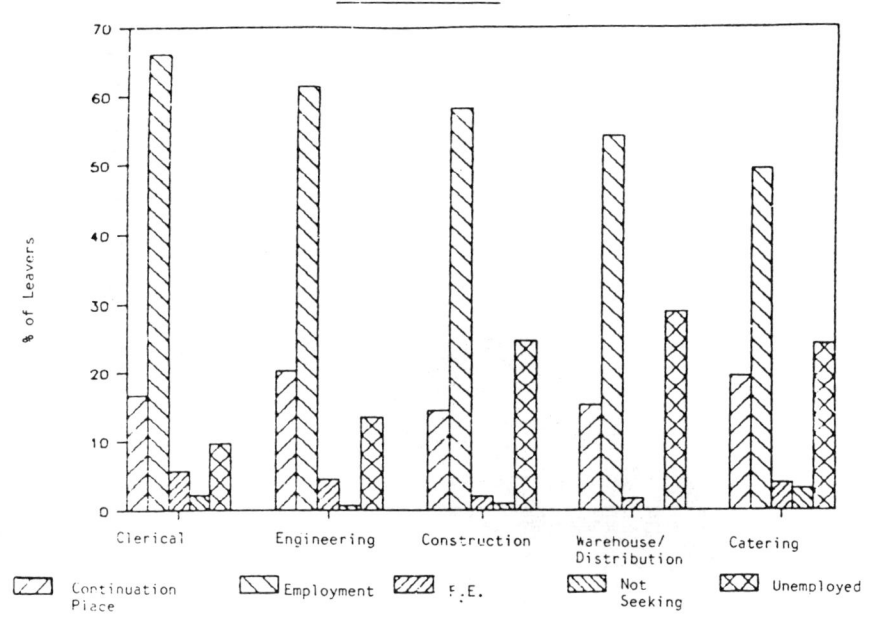

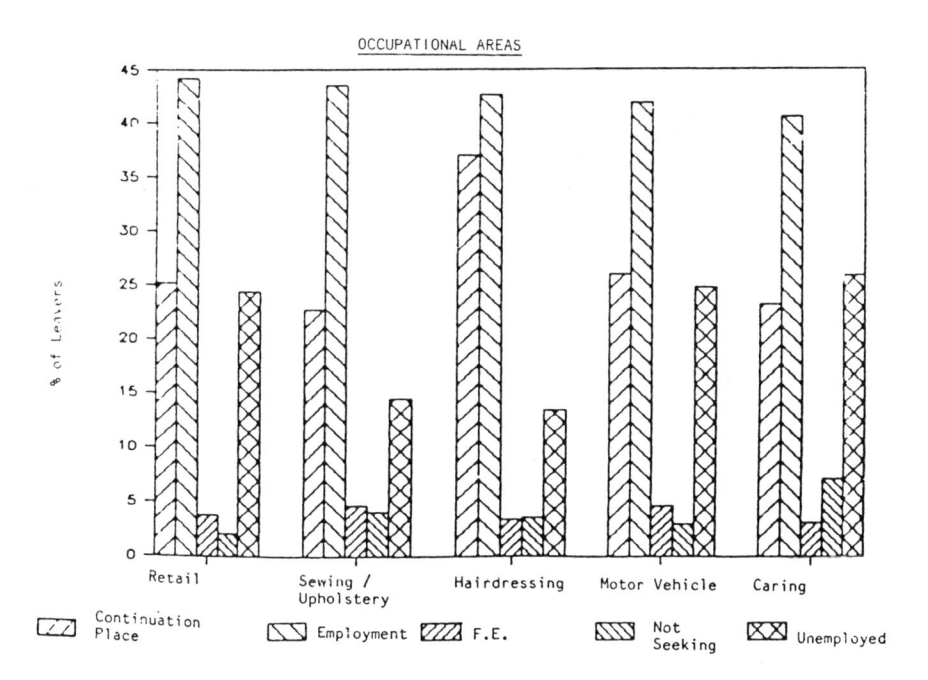

OCCUPATIONAL AREAS

DESTINATIONS OF 1986 FIFTH YEAR LEAVERS FROM MAINTAINED SCHOOLS IN EAST SUSSEX

- 6TH 34.9%
- FE 14%
- U/E 3.34%
- JOB 23.2%
- YTS 16.7%
- OTHER 7.92%

COMPARISON BETWEEN THE DESTINATIONS OF MALE AND FEMALE EAST SUSSEX FIFTH YEAR SCHOOL LEAVERS 1986

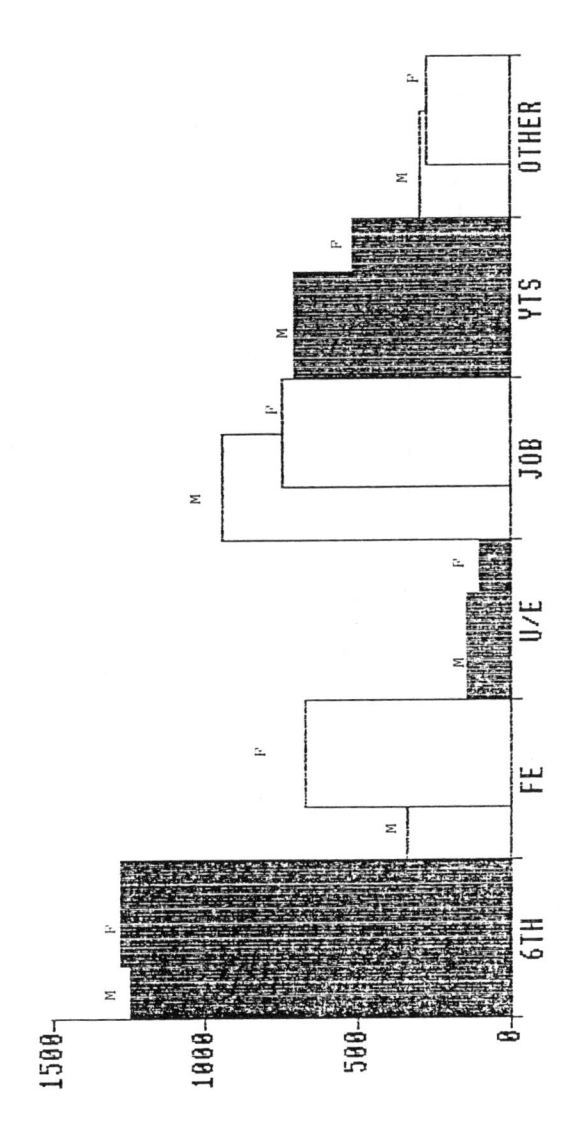

COMPARISON BETWEEN JOBS AND YTS PLACES ENTERED BY EAST SUSSEX 5TH YEAR SCHOOL-LEAVERS 1986 (as known at 1.10.86)

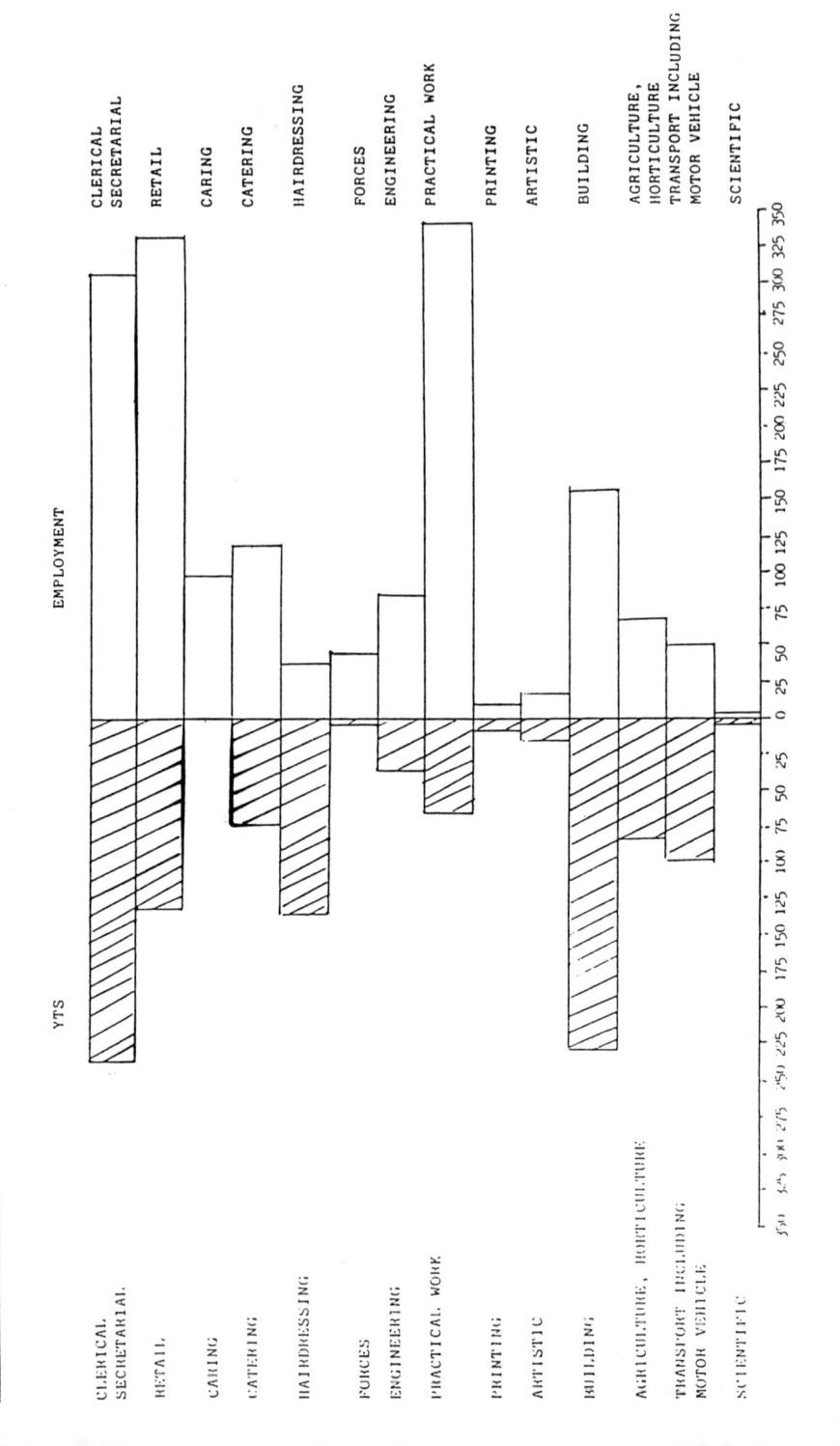

CITY OF BRADFORD METROPOLITAN COUNCIL
SCHOOL LEAVER STATISTICS FOR SCHOOL YEAR 1985/86

ANALYSIS OF PUPILS REACHING STATUTORY SCHOOL LEAVING AGE	MALE Indigenous	MALE Ethnic Minority	FEMALE Indigenous	FEMALE Ethnic Minority	TOTAL
Number reaching statutory school-leaving age.	2984	841	2972	651	7448
Number of these remaining at school	661	432	805	240	2138
Number of these leaving for FE	108	43	260	22	433
Number leaving for employment	2215	366	1907	389	4877
Number of these entering first employment	790	31	660	33	1514
Number of these registered as unemployed	282	109	211	118	720
Number of these entering Youth Training Scheme	907	136	746	129	1918
Number of these not registered	139	45	156	61	401
Number of these transferred to other areas	97	45	134	48	324
ANALYSIS OF VI FORM PUPILS					
Number leaving VI forms	740	423	802	236	2201
Number of these leaving for HE/FE	348	215	366	49	978
Number leaving for employment	392	208	436	187	1223
Number of these entering first employment	217	36	270	30	553
Number of these registered as unemployed	75	96	57	46	274
Number of these entering Youth Training Scheme	75	43	51	32	201
Number of these not registered	4	15	20	62	101
Number of these transferred to other areas	21	18	38	17	94
ANALYSIS OF THOSE WHO LEFT SCHOOL FOR HE/FE					
University	141	41	94	10	286
Polytechnic and other Higher Education	109	22	83	6	220
Technical College	206	195	449	55	905

TO SHOW DESTINATIONS OF SURREY FIFTH YEAR (1986)

Diagram 1

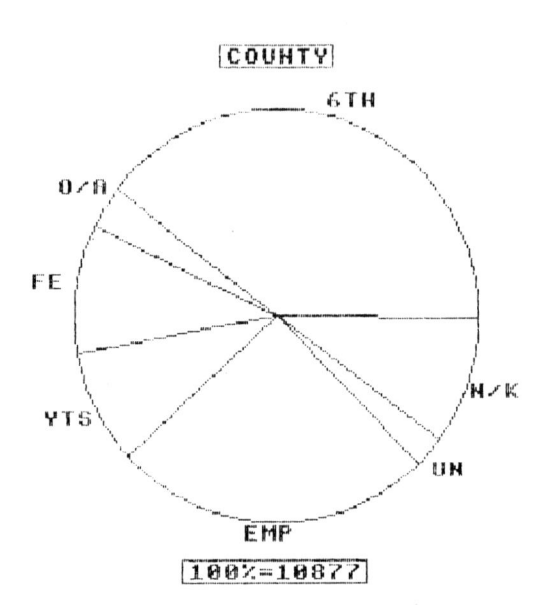

[COUNTY pie chart with segments: 6TH, O/A, FE, YTS, EMP, UN, N/K; 100%=10877]

Table 1

	Category	Number
1	Continuing General Education, at sixth form & sixth form college (6TH)	4285 (40%)
2	Continuing General Education at FE College (O/A)	362 (3%)
3	Starting vocational course at FE college (FE)	1095 (10%)
4	Starting training for Skills - YTS (YTS)	978 (9%)
5	Entering Employment (EMP)	2779 (25%)
6	Currently registered as unemployed (UN)	287 (3%)
7	Destination unknown (N/K)	1091 (10%)

Surrey
DIAGRAM 3
COMPARING NUMBERS OF FIFTH YEAR LEAVERS (1986) ENTERING EMPLOYMENT, FURTHER EDUCATION AND YTS

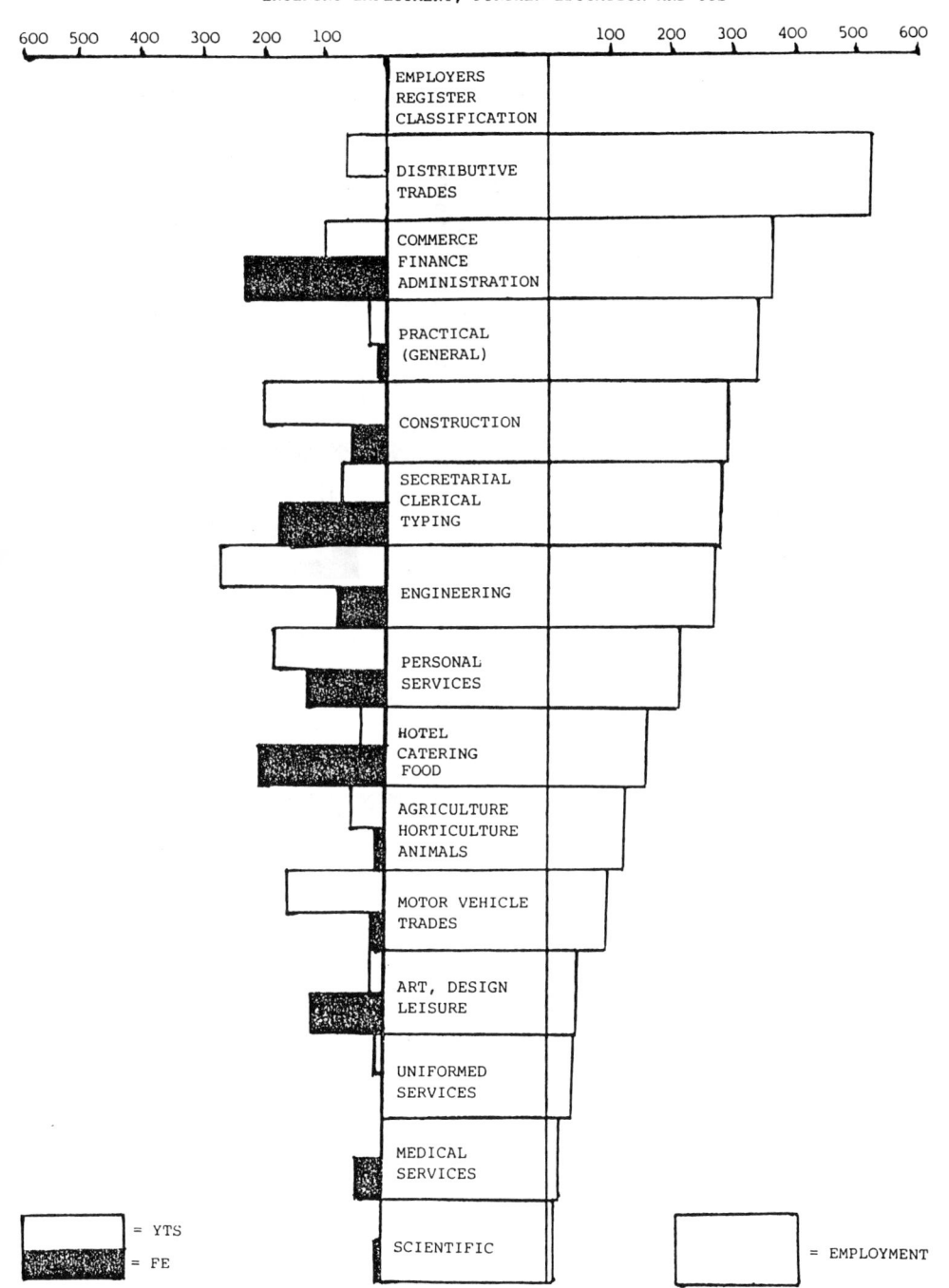

Categories (Employers Register Classification):
- DISTRIBUTIVE TRADES
- COMMERCE FINANCE ADMINISTRATION
- PRACTICAL (GENERAL)
- CONSTRUCTION
- SECRETARIAL CLERICAL TYPING
- ENGINEERING
- PERSONAL SERVICES
- HOTEL CATERING FOOD
- AGRICULTURE HORTICULTURE ANIMALS
- MOTOR VEHICLE TRADES
- ART, DESIGN LEISURE
- UNIFORMED SERVICES
- MEDICAL SERVICES
- SCIENTIFIC

Scale: 600 500 400 300 200 100 | 100 200 300 400 500 600

Legend:
- ☐ = YTS
- ▨ = FE
- ☐ = EMPLOYMENT

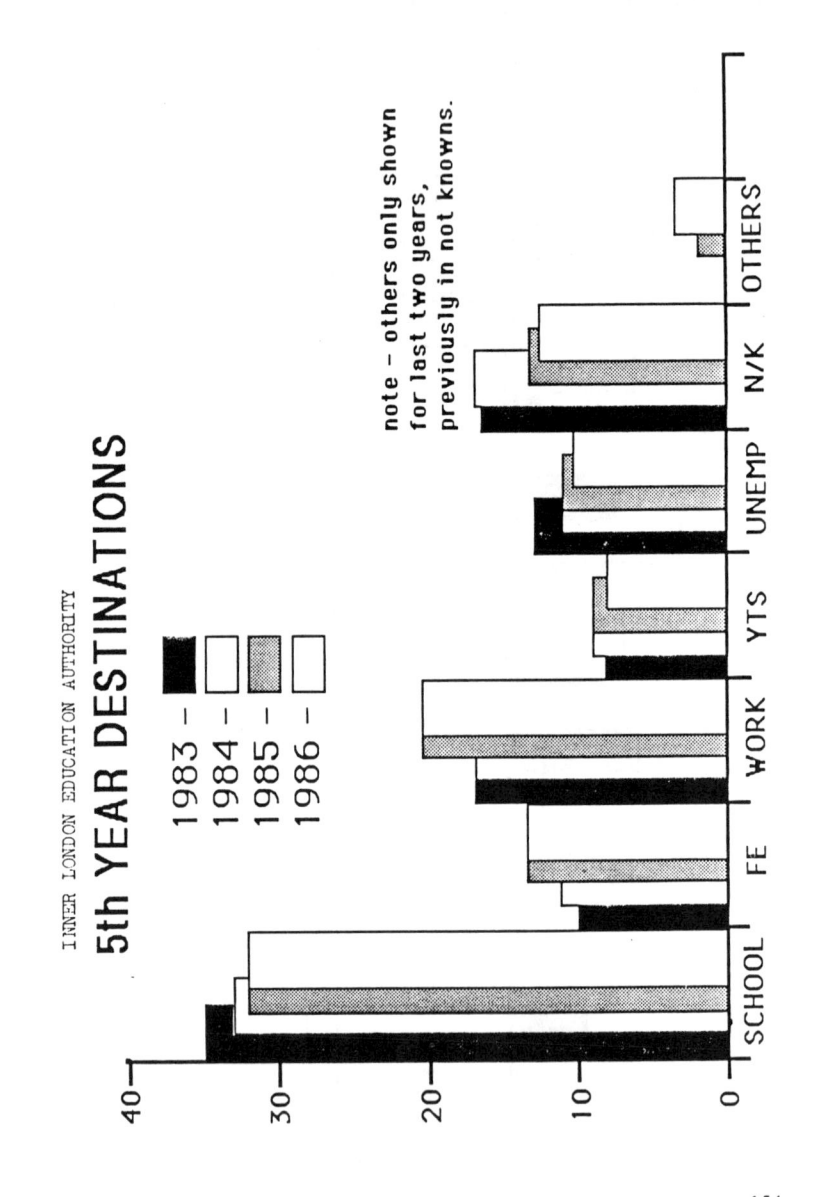

INNER LONDON EDUCATION AUTHORITY

5th YEAR DESTINATIONS

1983 –
1984 –
1985 –
1986 –

note – others only shown for last two years, previously in not knowns.

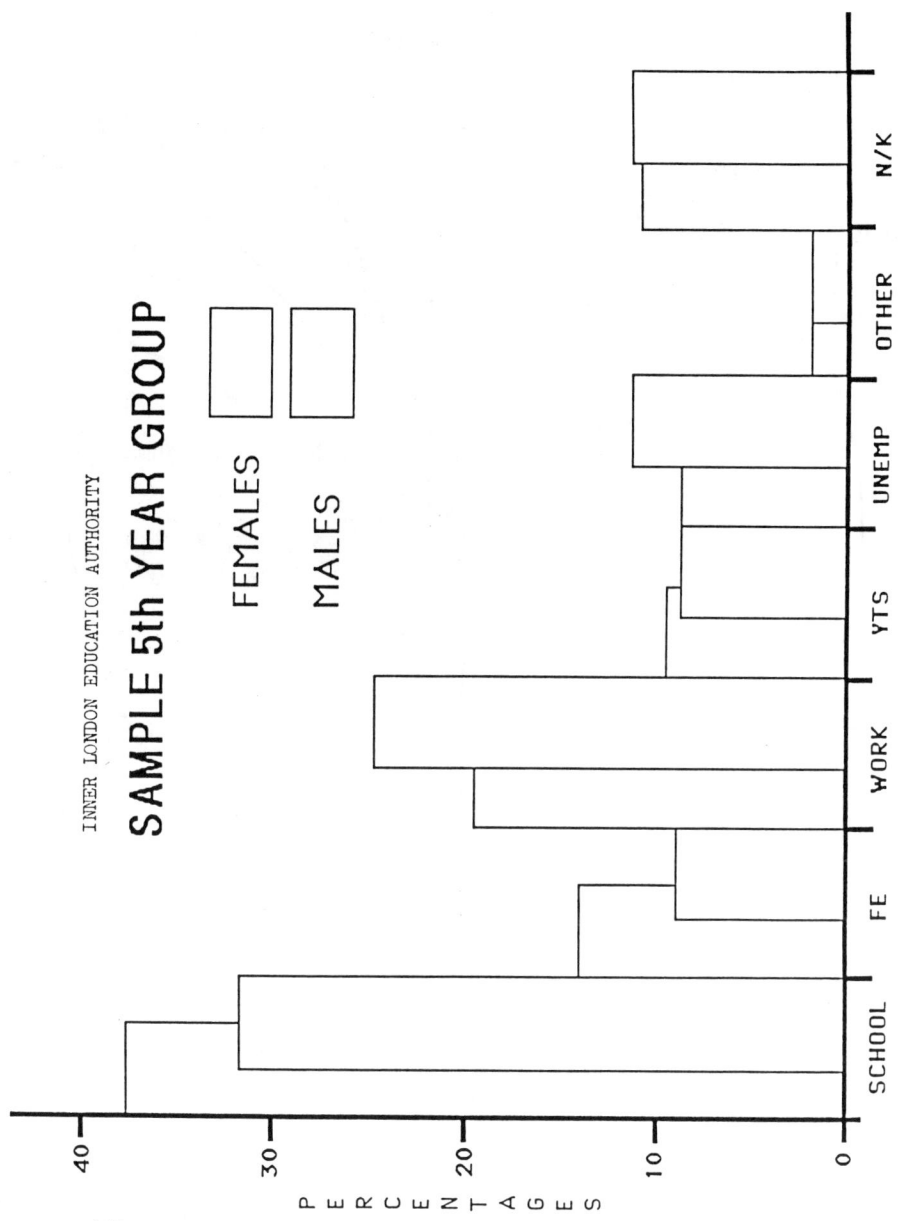

INNER LONDON EDUCATION AUTHORITY

SAMPLE 5th YEAR GROUP

FEMALES
MALES

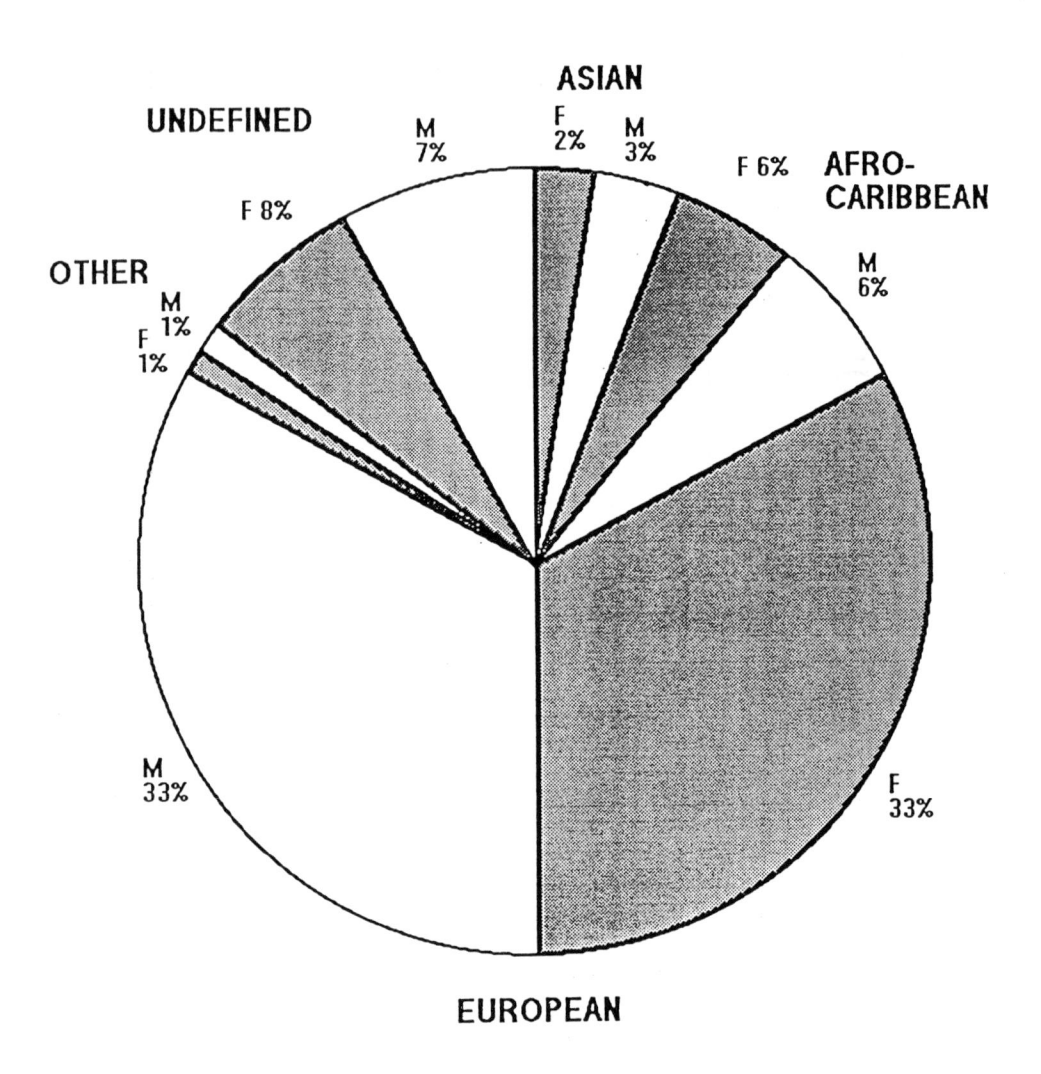

5th YEAR SAMPLE GROUP

INNER LONDON EDUCATION AUTHORITY

- ASIAN: F 2%, M 3%
- AFRO-CARIBBEAN: F 6%, M 6%
- EUROPEAN: F 33%, M 33%
- OTHER: F 1%, M 1%
- UNDEFINED: F 8%, M 7%

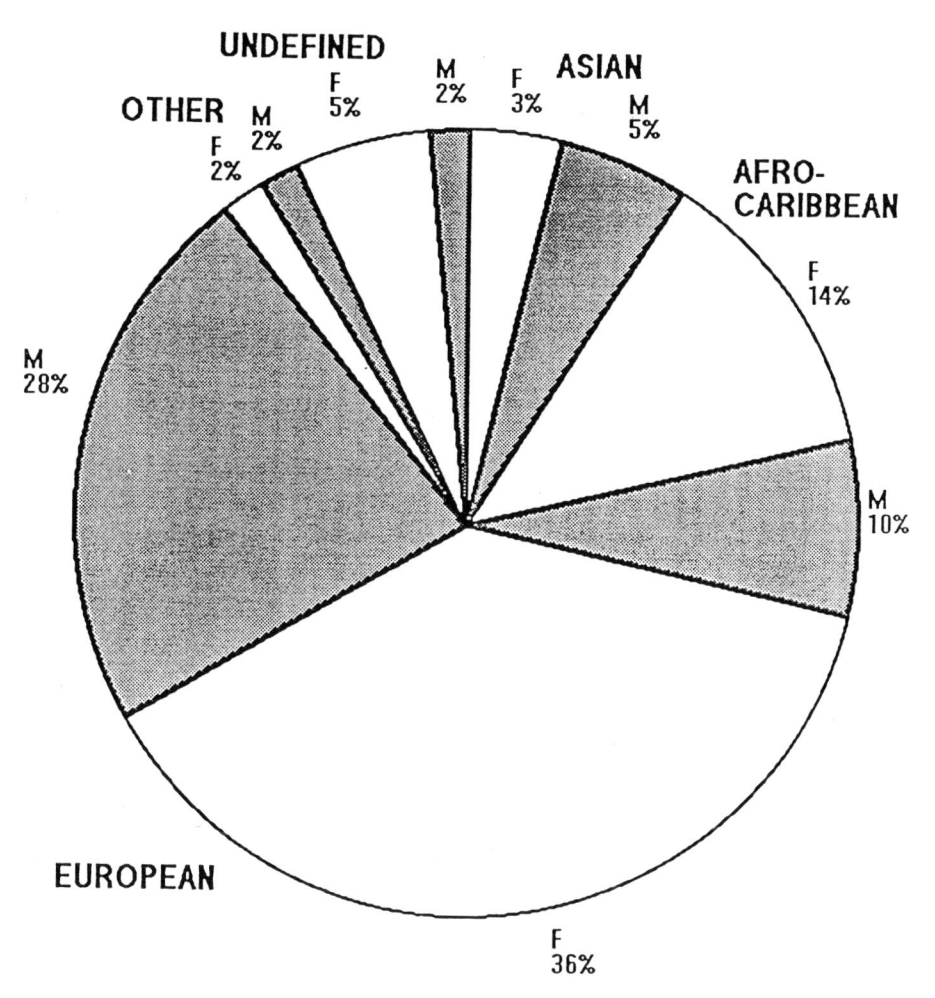

OTHER UNDEFINED ASIAN
F 2% M 2% F 5% M 2% F 3% M 5%

AFRO-CARIBBEAN
F 14%

M 28%

M 10%

EUROPEAN

F 36%

SAMPLE INTO FURTHER EDUCATION

INNER LONDON EDUCATION AUTHORITY